CHANGED
BY LOVE

CHANGED BY LOVE

*living a Spirit-filled life
in a self-centered world*

Ryan Sidhom

Changed By Love:
living a Spirit-filled life
in a self-centered world.
Copyright © 2024 Ryan Sidhom

This book is manufactured in the United States.

ISBN 979-8-3240-2899-2

Edited by Clarissa Sidhom and Vera Sidhom
Cover design by Clarissa Sidhom

DEDICATION

To Clarissa for her tireless support, late nights helping me with layout design and grammar lessons, proofreading, and watching the boys so I could get this done, and to constantly putting wind in my sails. To my mom, Vera, for encouraging me to keep going, and for helping with proofreading. To my boys, Banner and Anchor - you're going to change the world!

To my countless mentors, thanks for continuing to pour into me.

And to everybody who has been changed by love. This is for you!

Week 04

Week 05

Introduction

Hey! I'm Ryan, the pastor at River City Church in Vancouver, WA. I'm so excited that you are holding this book in your hands!

The fact that you have this book indicates two things:

1. You are a believer in Jesus (either newly, or for some time)
2. You are interested in growing your faith further

Both of these things are so exciting! If you're new to the faith, welcome to the family! If you're not new to the faith, welcome to the continued journey. Regardless of if you've been a believer for a week, or several decades, it is admirable that you are making the decision to grow your faith in an intentional way!

Here's my promise to you: If you faithfully read each day, you will be stretched and grown in new ways. You will grow to be more like Jesus. You will find your greater purpose in this life, and you will have fun doing it! Here are some pointers to get the most out of this book:

1. **Read this book with a highlighter.** There is a TON of information in this book, and some parts will be more relevant/applicable to your life than others. Be sure to have a way to mark what resonates with you.

2. **Read this book with a friend or mentor.** Meet on a weekly basis if possible to talk about what you're learning, and how you're applying it.

3. **Visit the "Thresholds" section often**. At the end of this book, there is a list of things that I am challenging you to complete by the time you finish this book. You can finish them in whatever order is easiest, but keep them on the forefront of your mind.

All for King Jesus! Cheers!

Blessings,
Ryan Sidhom
Pastor, River City Church in Vancouver, WA

Week 01

Being Sure of Your Salvation

We know that the gift of salvation (having our sins paid for and securing our eternity with Jesus in heaven after we die) is free, but it is not automatic. Like I mentioned in the previous book, *Curious?*, if I hand you a $20 bill, it's not automatically yours… you have to reach out and take it.

In order to "reach out and take" God's free gift of salvation, the Bible tells us that we have to do a few things:

> If you openly declare that Jesus is Lord and believe in your heart that God raised him from the dead, you will be saved.
> **Romans 10:9**

Believing in God is not enough. Simply trying to be a good person is not enough. Changing your online profile to say

"Christian" is not enough. You have to actually believe Jesus is Who He says He is, and that He did what He said He did.

In fact, check out what the Bible says about our salvation:

> God saved you by his grace when you believed. And you can't take credit for this; it is a gift from God. Salvation is not a reward for the good things we have done, so none of us can boast about it. For we are God's masterpiece. He has created us anew in Christ Jesus, so we can do the good things he planned for us long ago.
> **Ephesians 2:8-10**

Our salvation really has a lot less to do with us than it has to do with what God did for us. And although believing is a big part of it, we cannot stop at simple belief. James, the brother of Jesus, had something to say about people who simply "believed" but didn't do anything else:

> You say you have faith, for you believe that there is one God. Good for you! Even the demons believe this, and they tremble in terror. How foolish! Can't you see that faith without good deeds is useless?
> **James 2:19-20**

Our sin, which is what separates us from God, cannot be paid for by either good works or by simple belief. Our sins can only be paid for by the blood of Jesus.

And not only did Jesus' death on the cross pay the penalty for our sins, but Jesus' resurrection is what God uses to draw us near to Himself. Check out this verse:

> And this is what God has testified: He has given us eternal life, and this life is in his Son. Whoever has the Son has life; whoever does not have God's Son does not have life. I have written this to you who believe in the name of the Son of God, so that you may know you have eternal life.
>
> **1 John 5:11-13**

So, you being sure of your salvation really depends on how you answer this question: Who is Jesus to you?

Do you believe that Jesus is the Son of God?

Do you believe that He died a real death for your sins, and that He rose again from the grave, defeating the power of sin and death?

Do you believe that Jesus is also God in the flesh? And, in addition to all those things, are you trying to be more like Jesus?

If you answered "yes" to these questions, it's safe to say that you are a part of the family of God! Because the one and only way to get your sins forgiven is through the blood of Jesus–by accepting the blood payment that He made on the cross for your sins, and believing that He is who He says He is!

Simply put, if you trust in what Jesus did for you, and you keep your eyes on trying to be more like Him, then you're good!

Check out these really comforting words of Jesus:

> I give them eternal life, and they will never perish. No one can snatch them away from me.
> **John 10:28**

If you belong to Jesus, then He will not allow anything, or anyone, to snatch you out of His hands. You are His forever! And He will always be yours.

And when Jesus has something in His hands, you better be sure He wants to do something extra special with it.

Jesus has some pretty big plans for you!

Week 01, Day 02

Being Extra Sure

Being part of the family of God doesn't simply mean that we will live forever in heaven with Jesus after we die (although it does). It also means that we have the privilege of living our lives to bring a piece of heaven down to earth before we die!

The Kingdom of God in your life doesn't start in heaven…the Kingdom of God in your life starts the moment you become a part of the family. And because of that, we are able to start experiencing the results of a life with God right now.

The Bible refers to these experiences of a life with God as "fruits of the Spirit." They are called fruits because they are the things that the Spirit of God will produce in our lives to prove that we are Christians (like apples are how you prove a tree is an apple tree). Check out the fruits of the Spirit as listed in this verse:

> But the Holy Spirit produces this kind of fruit in our lives: love, joy, peace, patience, kindness, goodness, faithfulness, gentleness, and self-control. There is no law against these things!
> **Galatians 5:22-23**

Now, did you notice anything about this list of fruits of the Spirit? Besides the fact that they are all good things…they are all things that affect our relationship with those around us!

You see, like I mentioned already, belonging to the Kingdom of God is not all about us, but about bringing the Kingdom of God to earth. If you have begun to experience these new attitudes both inwardly and with your dealings with those around you, then that is a sign that you have truly been changed by love!

That is one way the Spirit of God confirms to our spirit that we belong to Him.

> For his Spirit joins with our spirit to affirm that we are God's children.
> **Romans 8:16**

When we start following Jesus, His Spirit comes and lives inside us, and we literally become a new person.

This means that anyone who belongs to Christ has become a new person. The old life is gone; a new life has begun! And all of this is a gift from God, who brought us back to himself through Christ. And God has given us this task of reconciling people to him.

2 Corinthians 5:17-18

Did you catch that last sentence? We have been given the task, or the mission, of reconciling people to God.

Reconciling…that's a big word that I don't usually hear unless we're talking about reconciling a check book, which we don't really use anymore, so yeah…let me explain that one.

Reconcile is an old war term that literally means two opposing and enemy parties becoming friends. Not simply a surrender, but like opposing gangs sitting down for tea together.

Because of sin, we were viewed as "enemies of God" until our sins were forgiven by Jesus. So, our job is to help enemies of God (people who are sinners, so *everybody*) become friends with God by letting them know about the Good News of Jesus!

And when Jesus reconciles us to God, it is final. There's no going back to being enemies. In fact, check out this Bible verse:

And I am convinced that nothing can ever separate us from God's love. Neither death nor life, neither angels nor demons, neither our fears for today nor our worries about tomorrow—not even the powers of hell can separate us from God's love. No power in the sky above or in the earth below—indeed, nothing in all creation will ever be able to separate us from the love of God that is revealed in Christ Jesus our Lord.

Romans 8:38-39

Nothing can separate us from Jesus anymore.

Not even future sins.

Don't get me wrong, people who belong to Jesus still struggle with sin. I still struggle with sin. You will still struggle with sin. But, when you accepted Jesus' blood payment for your sins, that meant payment for *all* of your sins (past, present, and future).

And so, if you are really serious about believing in Jesus, and what He did for you on the cross, and about following Him… then that means you have absolutely nothing to worry about!

You belong to Jesus, and Jesus belongs to you. You can rest easy tonight in the love of Jesus!

Week 01, Day 03

Living in the Spirit

When we become followers of Jesus, the Spirit of God Himself comes down to live within us, and to lead us and guide us. Kind of like the "angel on your shoulder" kind of thing, but much less cartoonish.

When we become followers of Jesus, our lives are changed from the inside out. Check out what Jesus said in the Book of John:

> And I will ask the Father, and he will give you another Advocate, who will never leave you. He is the Holy Spirit, who leads into all truth. The world cannot receive him, because it isn't looking for him and doesn't recognize him. But you know him, because he lives with you now and later will be in you.
> **John 14:16-17**

According to this passage, God the Father (we'll explore that concept later in Week 04, Day 01) sent down God the Holy Spirit (Week 04, Day 04) at the request of God the Son, Jesus (Week 04, Day 03). And one of the primary roles of God the Holy Spirit is to lead us to live our lives in Truth and in Love.

And, I don't know if you caught this or not…but that verse says the Spirit of God will never leave us. Ever.

Now, you might be wondering what the point of the Spirit of God is. I mean, we already have God and Jesus, why the Spirit as well?

Well, it's quite simple, really. You see, Jesus was God in human form. He came down to earth, and He lived among us. He walked, talked, ate, etc. But, as is the case with humans, He was only in one place at one time, and that was it.

When Jesus rose from the dead and ascended back into heaven, He sent down His Spirit to live among His believers all over the world—because spirits are not bound by time and space.

So, the same Spirit of God that lives inside you is living inside me right now. And, He's living in the believers in China right now. And, He's living in each and every believer on earth.
And where the Spirit of God is, He is leading in truth.

> When the Spirit of truth comes, he will guide you into all truth. He will not speak on his own but will tell you what he has heard. He will tell you about the future. He will bring me glory by telling you whatever he receives from me. All that belongs to the Father is mine; this is why I said, 'The Spirit will tell you whatever he receives from me.'
>
> **John 16:13-15**

Now, that leads me to something else entirely…does that mean that Christians are always speaking the Truth? Always? And does that mean that whatever Christians believe is the Truth? Always? And does that mean that Christians cannot ever be wrong?

Not at all.

First things first, keep in mind that all Christians are still sinners. So, there are many times when Christians accidentally slip back into sin (it's a constant struggle). But, in addition to the sin issue, Christians are not necessarily always following the leadership or the guidance of the Spirit of God.

> Here's a good Bible verse to keep tucked away:
> Don't be drunk with wine, because that will ruin your life. Instead, be filled with the Holy Spirit.
>
> **Ephesians 5:18**

Why would we need instructions to be filled with the Spirit if we are all automatically filled with the Spirit once we become a Christian?

I'm glad you asked! Because…that's a misconception.

Just because we *receive* the Spirit of God when we become believers does not mean that we are always *filled* with His Spirit.

It's not a one-time thing. We are called to constantly be filling ourselves up with the Spirit of God. And this is a command, not a recommendation or simply a suggestion.

"Be filled with the Spirit."

You see…*possessing* the Spirit of God, and being *filled* with the Spirit of God are entirely different things.

When we are filled with the Spirit of God like **Ephesians 5:18** commands us to do, that means we are coming under control of the Spirit of God. And that's not something that automatically happens. Because we are still humans, and because we still have sin natures, there are times when we follow those desires and instincts (referred to in the Bible as "the flesh") instead of following the Spirit of God.

Like my mentor once told me: every Christian is a walking civil war. We've got to choose daily which side we will serve.

So at any given time, we as Christians are either being controlled by our flesh (and probably sinning), or being controlled by the Spirit of God, and living out His desire for our lives.

> So I say, let the Holy Spirit guide your lives. Then you won't be doing what your sinful nature craves. The sinful nature wants to do evil, which is just the opposite of what the Spirit wants. And the Spirit gives us desires that are the opposite of what the sinful nature desires. These two forces are constantly fighting each other, so you are not free to carry out your good intentions.
> **Galatians 5:16-17**

When we are under the control of the Spirit of God, the Spirit allows us to live like Jesus.

When we are controlled by the flesh, we live like our old selves. So, you may be wondering how to make sure we are controlled by the Spirit of God instead of being controlled by our flesh. And honestly, it's simple…but it's not always easy.

You start by literally praying, "God, fill me with Your Spirit today.

Fill me with Your Spirit this hour. Allow me to keep my eyes on You, and to live like Jesus would. Empower me to make decisions that are honoring to You. Keep me strong enough to stay away from the sins that tempt me daily."

Pray that prayer today. And again tomorrow. And the next day.

Say that prayer this hour. And again in another hour. And then again in two hours from now.

Simple…but not easy.

But when you pray for God's Spirit to control you and lead you and guide you, He will. And as long as you stay focused on Him, He will keep you faithful.

But be warned–civil wars are the ones that hurt the most.

Stand strong, but remember that Jesus forgives you when you fail.

Week 01, Day 04

Living in the Spirit, Part 2

When Jesus was spending time with His disciples after His resurrection, He gave them a sneak peek of what was coming:

> "Do not leave Jerusalem until the Father sends you the gift he promised, as I told you before. John baptized with water, but in just a few days you will be baptized with the Holy Spirit."
> **Acts 1:4b-5**

And when Jesus was having His last conversation with His disciples while He was here on earth, this is what He said:

> But you will receive power when the Holy Spirit comes upon you. And you will be my witnesses, telling people

about me everywhere—in Jerusalem, throughout Judea, in Samaria, and to the ends of the earth."
Acts 1:8

The disciples lived and did ministry with Jesus for three years, but no amount of training, even from the "Master Trainer," was enough. Instead of taking the world by storm, the disciples were instructed to…wait.

Wait until the Holy Spirit comes down, because they could not do this without the power that He would bring.

That had to be a really frustrating thing for the disciples to hear, but at the same time, it had to be so encouraging. Jesus was leaving, but He promised that His Spirit was still going to be among them. And not just the presence of Jesus through His Spirit, but the *power* of Jesus through His Spirit!

And that promise is not just for those first century followers of Jesus. It's extended to all followers of Jesus across time and geography! This promise is for you and for me as well!

I don't know about you, but that gets me so pumped up and excited! It makes me want to go take on the world for Jesus! But…I'd be foolish to do it without the power of the Spirit.

God the Father is using God the Holy Spirit to draw us nearer and nearer to God the Son, Jesus, every single day that we'll allow Him to. Not only that, but the Spirit of God is also working in the lives of those around us, as they see the reflection of Jesus in our lives.

The Spirit of God is a pretty powerful person!

As you continue to read this book and act in obedience, you may notice people around you that are not yet believers in Jesus start to ask some deep questions. This is not a coincidence.

As people start to see more and more of Jesus in you, the Holy Spirit of God will draw them closer, and give them some good questions to ask. As you notice this happening, I challenge you to begin to make a list of these people for the purpose of praying for them, and being intentional with telling them about Who it is you are really following.

Some of these people might even be a good candidate to read through *Curious?* together with!

Keep this in mind: one of the main functions of God the Holy Spirit is to bring people closer to God the Son, Jesus. And if you are constantly filled with God the Holy Spirit, then you better believe that He is going to use you to help people move closer to Jesus! He is going to use you to help people walk from spiritual death to spiritual life!

But remember this…just like the disciples of Jesus had to wait for the power of the Holy Spirit, the same is true of us. No amount of training or knowledge will ever replace the power of the Holy Spirit of God moving and working within us and through us.

So, just like we talked about yesterday, don't forget to pray today to ask the Holy Spirit to fill you and to use you for His glory.

And don't forget to do it tomorrow, as well.

When you are praying for the Holy Spirit to fill you, go ahead and ask the Holy Spirit to also lead you to those who really need to hear the good news of Jesus.

Pray that the Holy Spirit will use you to impart hope to them.

Be prepared to discuss this idea this week with the person who you are reading this book through with.

All for King Jesus!

Week 01, Day 05

The Importance of Baptism

Shortly before Jesus ascended into heaven, He gave His disciples some final marching orders. The final marching orders are commonly referred to as "The Great Commission." We are going to cover this more fully in Week 06, Day 01, but Jesus said:

> "I have been given all authority in heaven and on earth. Therefore, go and make disciples of all the nations, baptizing them in the name of the Father and the Son and the Holy Spirit. Teach these new disciples to obey all the commands I have given you. And be sure of this: I am with you always, even to the end of the age."
> **Matthew 28:18b-20**

In this Great Commission is the command for new disciples to be baptized in the name of God the Father, God the Son, and

God the Holy Spirit. As a new disciple (follower) of Jesus, this is an important step for you to take.

This is something that Jesus said should be done all across the world ("of all nations"), as well as all across time ("even to the end of the age"). So, if nothing else, baptism is an important thing to do because it is something that Jesus commanded.

Part of the importance of baptism is to indicate the inner change that has taken place within us, as well as to display our unity with other people across the globe who have also chosen to follow Jesus. Check out this verse:

> Some of us are Jews, some are Gentiles, some are slaves, and some are free. But we have all been baptized into one body by one Spirit, and we all share the same Spirit.
> **1 Corinthians 12:13**

But it's important to note that baptism is only an outward depiction of something that has happened inwardly. Baptism doesn't make you a follower of Jesus, it only indicates that this is a decision that you have made.

It is a way for you to identify with the rest of those who have chosen to follow Jesus. But not only are we identifying with other believers in Jesus, but we are actually identifying with Jesus Himself through the act of baptism.

Allow me to explain.

To start, you need to understand that different churches do baptism in different ways. Some choose to "sprinkle" or pour water on top of someone's head and call it baptism. Other churches choose to actually get in a giant bathtub-type thing, and to completely "submerge" or "immerse" each individual under the water.

While both types of baptism can be used as "identifiers" with other believers across the globe, it is the baptism by "immersion" where we truly see the identification with Jesus.

When we are dunked under the water, that represents our spiritual death. Through that, we are dying to our flesh (old way of living). We are also identifying with the death of Jesus on the cross for our sins.

While we are under water, we are identifying with Jesus, as His body was buried after death.

When we are lifted back up out of the water, that represents our resurrection to new spiritual life! In our new spiritual life, we are saying that we will choose to live our lives full of the Holy Spirit, while rejecting the way that we used to live. It is through this that we are also identifying with Jesus' resurrection from the dead!

So when we are baptized, we are claiming this truth in our lives:

> My old self has been crucified with Christ. It is no longer I who live, but Christ lives in me. So I live in this earthly body by trusting in the Son of God, who loved me and gave himself for me.
> **Galatians 2:20**

I like to say that baptism is similar to a team jersey. Because I'm in Vancouver, WA, we have a lot of Seattle Seahawks fans up here. Every time I see somebody with a Seattle Seahawks jersey, it would be ridiculous for me to assume that they actually played for the Seahawks!

Just because you have a jersey, doesn't mean you're really on the team. Sometimes the person wearing the jersey is simply a fan of the team.

Jesus isn't looking for people who will sit in the stands and watch. Jesus is looking for people who are willing to get on the field and actually play the game.

Baptism doesn't make you part of the Kingdom of God any more than a jersey makes you the quarterback of your favorite NFL team. Because honestly, the majority of people with the quarterback's jersey are simply spectators.

What makes you a part of the team is actually getting recruited.

If you choose to follow Jesus, that is your recruitment! And the Holy Spirit has begun to teach you the playbook through many different experiences.

And after you're recruited…you better believe you're not just simply going to start learning the playbook, but you're going to receive that jersey as well (baptism).

And when people see that you've been recruited (following Jesus) and that you've got the jersey (baptism), and that you're learning the playbook (living in the Spirit), there will be no question as to what team you're playing for!

So…let's talk about getting you fitted for a jersey!

Week 01, Day 06

What the Bible Says About Baptism

As we discussed in yesterday's reading, baptism is something that we see primarily reserved for people who believe in Jesus. I say "primarily" because the Bible also talks about something called "The baptism of John."

For instance, Paul (the greatest missionary and starter of churches mentioned in the New Testament) came across some people on this one occasion:

> While Apollos was in Corinth, Paul traveled through the interior regions until he reached Ephesus, on the coast, where he found several believers. "Did you receive the Holy Spirit when you believed?" he asked them.

"No," they replied, "we haven't even heard that there is a Holy Spirit."

"Then what baptism did you experience?" he asked.

And they replied, "The baptism of John."

Paul said, "John's baptism called for repentance from sin. But John himself told the people to believe in the one who would come later, meaning Jesus."

As soon as they heard this, they were baptized in the name of the Lord Jesus.
Acts 19:1-5

So, according to this passage, getting baptized *before* you receive the Holy Spirit of God (before you believe in Jesus) is not good enough. And if that's what you did, that's ok…but you should be baptized again, now that you believe in Jesus!

Another thing that the Bible makes clear is that baptism is the first act of obedience after choosing to follow Jesus. Time after time, we see people being baptized "immediately" after believing.

Then Peter continued preaching for a long time, strongly urging all his listeners, "Save yourselves from this crooked generation!"

Those who believed what Peter said were baptized and added to the church that day—about 3,000 in all.
Acts 2:40-41

3,000 believed and were baptized on the *same day*. If that's not enough to convince you, check out what happened when a gentile (non-Jewish) person named Cornelius believed:

So he (Peter) gave orders for them (Cornelius & friends) to be baptized in the name of Jesus Christ. Afterward Cornelius asked him to stay with them for several days.
Acts 10:48

And finally, here's what Ananias (a believer) said to Saul (literally, a terrorist) once he believed:

"What are you waiting for? Get up and be baptized. Have your sins washed away by calling on the name of the Lord."
Acts 22:16

There are many other examples, but I think you get the point. We've looked at what the Bible says baptism is (and the difference between the baptism of John and Christian baptism), who the Bible says should get baptized, and when. So, let's talk about why and how.

We've already discussed some of the "why," but I want to point out this important verse about identifying with Jesus:

> For you were buried with Christ when you were baptized. And with him you were raised to new life because you trusted the mighty power of God, who raised Christ from the dead.
>
> **Colossians 2:12**

And finally, check out this passage about when Philip (a faithful but "normal/everyday" believer like you or me) was living his life full of the Spirit. The Spirit of God led him on a journey to go talk to an Ethiopian eunuch (someone who had been castrated specifically for service to the Ethiopian queen). Philip got in the chariot that the Ethiopian eunuch was riding in and explained the Gospel (good news of Jesus) to him. And then this happened:

> As they rode along, they came to some water, and the eunuch said, "Look! There's some water! Why can't I be baptized?" "You can," Philip answered, "if you believe with all your heart." And the eunuch replied, "I believe that Jesus Christ is the Son of God." He ordered the carriage to stop, and they went down into the water, and Philip baptized him.
>
> **Acts 8:36-38**

I love this passage, because it clearly points out the order: believe and then be baptized. But when we're talking about the "how," the Bible doesn't give explicit instructions.

We know from the Great Commission that baptism should be done in the name of the Father, the Son, and the Holy Spirit. Those are clear instructions. But as far as "sprinkle" versus "immerse," the Bible doesn't give clear instructions.

What the Bible does provide, though, is clear examples.

In every example of baptism found in the Bible, it is done by immersion. We never see an example of someone being "sprinkled" in the Bible and the Bible calling it "baptism."

In addition to that, the Greek word (the original language the New Testament was written in) for baptize is βαπτίζω. Is that enough to convince you?) :)

This Greek word, pronounced "bap-teez-oh" is literally translated as "immerse" elsewhere in the Bible. So…there's that.

Bottom line, if you are a believer in Jesus and have not yet been baptized, I think it's time for you to get baptized! Talk to your pastor, church leader, or Christian mentor about next steps.

Week 01, Day 07

Next Steps for Baptism

To put it very simply, choosing not to get baptized is choosing to disobey Jesus. Baptism is the first public act of obedience that somebody should take after becoming a believer in Jesus.

"But what are some practical next steps I need to take before getting baptized?"

I'm glad you asked.

1. Talk to your pastor, church leader, or Christian mentor.

Baptism is not something that you can do in isolation. While there is no evidence in Scripture that a pastor has to baptize you instead of just a "normal" person who is a leader in your church, there is also no evidence of anybody ever being baptized without at least someone else there with them.

For instance, in yesterday's passage about Philip and the Ethiopian eunuch, Philip was a normal, everyday believer much like you and me. And, as far as we know, the only people present were Philip and the guy getting baptized.

Although this is not the norm (private baptisms), it is at least mentioned in Scripture—so it can't be wrong. But typically, baptisms were more of a public thing…like when 3,000 were baptized on the same day, probably with a crowd even larger than that watching.

But in every instance we see in Scripture, it involves someone that also believes doing the baptizing. Basically…you can't just sit in a dunk tank and get baptized by some punk kid with a good arm.

2. Affirm your faith

Very simply, baptism does not wash your sins away. Only Jesus can wash your sins away. So, be sure that your faith is in the right place (Jesus).

Chances are, the person baptizing you might ask you a few simple, but public questions before dunking you.

When we are baptizing people at River City Church in Vancouver, WA, we ask these two simple questions:

1. Do you believe that Jesus is the Son of God, and that He died to save you from your sins?
2. Are you going to follow Jesus for the rest of your days?

You don't want to be thinking through these questions for the very first time while you're about to be baptized. It is better that you've already thought through these things, and confirmed them in your mind and in your heart.

3. Set a date

Work together with the Christian leader who is going to be baptizing you, and finalize the date. I've known several people who are like, "I'm going to get baptized…someday."

Well guess what? They still haven't done it.

It's important to set a date, and make it happen. I understand some nervousness may be involved, but it really is exciting and important!

4. Invite your friends

This is an important and exciting event in your life! Some people who are close to you should be there to celebrate with you! And

I'm not just talking about other Christians…invite your friends who are not Christians as well!

If they are a friend, they'll probably be excited for you and with you, even if they don't fully understand what is happening, or why you're doing it. Plus, it might give you a good chance to share with your friends why you're doing it, and what you believe, and how Jesus is absolutely worth believing in and following!

How cool would it be for your non-believing friends to see you get baptized, ask some good questions, go through the *Curious?* book with you, and then maybe even believe and then get baptized…by you!

That, to me, sounds like such a beautiful story!

5. Wear a dark colored shirt when getting baptized

Just trying to save you some embarrassment.

If you're connected to River City Church, let's get you baptized and let's check off that "Get baptized" item in the "Thresholds" section in your copy of this book!

Week 02

Your Jesus Story

Every believer has a Jesus story (sometimes called a "testimony") worth sharing. And Jesus wants us to share that story with our friends, our families, our coworkers, and other people in our lives. But…there are certain ways to go about sharing your story in an appropriate and impactful way.

Chances are, you're reading this book in part because somebody shared their Jesus story with you at some point in time! It didn't stop with them, and Jesus doesn't want your story to stop with you. People have been sharing their Jesus stories for 2,000 years (since Jesus left earth), and faithful people will continue to share them until the end of time!

Imagine with me for one second that you discovered the cure for cancer, or the cure for AIDS…there is no way you'd ever dream of keeping that information to yourself! Doing so would be pretty selfish, to say the very least.

Check out this Bible verse:

> When Adam sinned, sin entered the world. Adam's sin brought death, so death spread to everyone, for everyone sinned. But there is a great difference between Adam's sin and God's gracious gift. For the sin of this one man, Adam, brought death to many. But even greater is God's wonderful grace and his gift of forgiveness to many through this other man, Jesus Christ. And the result of God's gracious gift is very different from the result of that one man's sin. For Adam's sin led to condemnation, but God's free gift leads to our being made right with God, even though we are guilty of many sins. For the sin of this one man, Adam, caused death to rule over many. But even greater is God's wonderful grace and his gift of righteousness, for all who receive it will live in triumph over sin and death through this one man, Jesus Christ.
> **Romans 5:12, 15-17**

Now, imagine with me that you discovered the cure for sin and spiritual death. Oh wait…you have! And keeping it to yourself would be pretty selfish, to say the least.

As a follower of Jesus, you are a disciple. And one of the things that Jesus wants is for His disciples to make more disciples. A disciple of Jesus who makes other disciples of Jesus is called a "disciple-maker." Jesus' desire for us is for every single one of us to get to the point in our lives where we could be considered a disciple-maker.

Jesus wants that from me, and Jesus wants that from you. And, although that may sound like a daunting task, the good news is that you are not alone on this journey! Looking back at the Great Commission (**Matthew 28:18-20**), Jesus said, "I am with you always, even to the end of the age." So…that's pretty much all the backup you need! Additionally, you've got the person you are reading this book with. And finally, you have me. Text me any time you need encouragement in the journey!
360.836.0639

Jesus wants you to share your Jesus story. He is with you, and if you're obedient in this manner, God will bless you for it!

Not only will God bless you for it, but you'll be able to be a blessing to others. And in addition to that, you will stand out as the minority of believers who are actually living out this command from Jesus (insert some survey about how most people who claim to be Christians don't act like Christians, *especially* when the barista gets their drink wrong).

So we are Christ's ambassadors; God is making his appeal through us. We speak for Christ when we plead, "Come back to God!"

2 Corinthians 5:20

An ambassador is somebody who goes to a place that is not their home to be a representative of their home (for instance, the U.S. Ambassador to Germany is a United States citizen who represents the U.S. while living abroad in Germany).

And here's the thing about this world we live in…

For this world is not our permanent home; we are looking forward to a home yet to come.

Hebrews 13:14

Our home is with Jesus in heaven. But until the point when we are home, we are called to be ambassadors for Jesus here on earth. And one of the primary ways you can be an effective ambassador is to share your Jesus story.

I know that this sounds intimidating. You might not have any idea where to start.

That's ok. We'll talk about that tomorrow!

Week 02, Day 02

Sharing Your Jesus Story

The very first step to sharing your Jesus story with somebody you know is…to listen to their story first!

I know this is probably not what you were expecting, but it is vitally important (and honestly, way less intimidating than busting out of the gate with your story). Listening to somebody else's story before you jump into your own allows for a couple things:

1. Understanding

If you haven't yet heard their story, you'll be surprised at how well you don't know somebody whom you think you know. And typically, people are excited to share their unique story, their life experiences, and their past or present struggles. The better understanding you have of their life experiences, the better you'll be prepared to share about how following Jesus can change their life and make it better!

2. Trust

There is something about listening to somebody's story that really builds trust with them. And when I say listening, I mean really, actively, intentionally listening.

Listening with interest.

It's pretty easy to tell when somebody isn't really listening to what you say. Maybe instead of listening, they are trying to think of what they're going to say next, or they're reading texts, or they're thinking about something else entirely, like what's for dinner.

Don't do that. When you are listening to somebody's story, keep in mind that they are being vulnerable with you. And, if you listen with interest and intentionality, that will build further trust in that relationship, which will lead to them being more interested in what you have to say.

After you have effectively listened to their story, then there may be a natural segue into you sharing you story. Keep in mind that all of this might not happen in the same sitting…but typically, when you've spent adequate time listening to somebody's experiences, there's going to come a point when they'll want to hear something from you.

If they don't, then you can ask some good questions that may lead into you sharing your story. For instance: "Wow, that's a really interesting story…do you have time for me to share a part of my story with you?"

If you have the opportunity to share, here are some tips that I've found make for an impactful story:

1. Before Jesus

There was a point in your life when you were not yet a follower of Jesus. This may have been recently, or it may have been several years ago. Regardless, share briefly about some of the things you experienced before you started following Jesus.

Keep in mind, you've just heard *some* of their story. As you're actively listening to their story, take note of things that you can relate to. Take note of similarities between your stories.

This would be a good time to share those similarities. For example, "There was a time when I was really feeling rejected as well, and similar to how you mentioned, I was struggling with finding a true and fulfilling purpose for my life. I didn't understand the reason why I was put here on earth."

Although you want to start with this "Before Jesus" section, you don't want to spend too much time in this section. The world is negative enough, and your friend probably has multiple sources of negativity in their life. They don't need more negativity.

They need hope!

2. Hope!

"Then there came a point in my journey where I actually found the hope I was looking for, and I found it in following Jesus! Since I've started following Jesus, I've found a real purpose for my life, and I've found acceptance, and family!"

Something along those lines. But be careful not to say it if it isn't true of your own life. You want to be sure to set a standard for really sharing truth. If you get sloppy with the truth, then chances are, they will be hesitant to believe you when you start sharing Truth ("truth" being your truth, "Truth" with a capital T being the Truth of Jesus, and what He has done for us!)

3. And since that point...

How has your life been different since then?

"Now that I'm living with this new purpose, I no longer feel aimless. Now that I'm living in this new relationship with Jesus, I no longer feel like I'm worthless."

Focus on the truth of how Jesus has changed your life! And if possible, make it relevant to the story that you've heard them share about their own experiences and struggles.

4. Pray

Beyond keeping up with the relationship (be sure to let your friend know that you value them, even if they don't choose to start following Jesus on the spot), you need to shift your focus to prayer. And I'm not talking about on the spot, but when you go home.

One of the beautiful things about our assignment from Jesus is He just asks us to share. It is not our job to convince anybody, and it is especially not our job to get into any argument or debate (those usually move people further away).

If you've shared your Jesus story with them in a relevant way, then you've been faithful! Rest in the truth that Jesus is proud of you, even if they didn't fall on their knees with arms raised to heaven in the middle of the coffee shop…journeys, especially significant ones, take time.

But, if the comfort level is right within the relationship, maybe you could offer to actually pray for them. One thing that I've found effective is saying this: "I'm not sure what you think about prayer, but I believe it is a powerful thing. When I am praying tonight, is there anything that I can be praying for you about?"

Typically, that catches people off guard, in a good way. Even if they don't believe what we believe, the fact that we are willing to take time out of our day to bring their requests before our God is a pretty significant thing.

If your friend is interested in learning more about Jesus, but is not ready to make any kind of commitment, here's another idea. What if you suggested that you guys read through *Curious?* together, and continue to meet on a weekly basis to further your relationship, and discuss what you are reading?

If this is something that you are interested in doing, text me if you need help getting a copy of the book! 360.836.0639

Week 02, Day 03

God's Story of Redemption

There are many effective ways to share God's story of redemption (the Gospel), but I'm going to focus on two. First of all, there is something called the "Romans Road." It is basically just a bunch of verses from the Book of Romans that very clearly explain the path to freedom in Jesus!

If you are interested in learning the "Romans Road," you can learn it by studying Week 10, Day 02 in the previous book, *Curious?*. It is pretty easy to remember (especially if you've got a Bible handy, or you can just highlight those verses in the Bible on your phone), and it is pretty easy to explain once you fully grasp it. So...go take a look, and see if that works well for you.

Remember, there's no "wrong way" to share God's story of Redemption (other than lying about it). So...if the Romans Road resonates well with you, then by all means use it. But, if you're looking for something else, I want to share with you another method called "Three Circles."

Keep in mind that the example that I'm about to give you of "Three Circles" should not be copied word for word, but should be personalized both for you, and the person you are sharing it with (after you've listened to their story).

Here's the big idea (and a good verse to memorize):

> For this is how God loved the world: He gave his one and only Son, so that everyone who believes in him will not perish but have eternal life.
> **John 3:16**

When you share God's story, keep in mind that it should be more of a "conversation," and less of a "presentation." Just like you probably don't like it when people "talk at you," God's story is more effectively shared when your friend can respond and ask questions, or maybe even answer questions that you ask.

An easy way to begin this conversation is by asking, "Can I show you a drawing that illustrates something that changed my life?" If they say yes, then let's go!

Grab a napkin or some other piece of paper, and draw a circle in the top right-hand corner. On top of the circle, write the word "brokenness." Say something like "I think we'd both agree that the world is a broken place." Then, put three words that describe the world's brokenness in the middle of that circle. You can ask for their input, or maybe even show that you were really listening to their story by using words that they used in their story.

For example, words like abuse, murder, suicide, global warming, selfishness, greed, racism, disease/sickness, and whatever else you can think of that is negative, and is a result of sin.

Then, draw three "squiggly" arrows coming out of the right side of the circle, pointing to the right. These arrows represent escapes. Again, use examples from their story, ask for their feedback, or simply fill in words like alcohol, drugs, giving to charity, going to church, volunteering, unhealthy relationships, money, education, and whatever else you can think of that people try to use as escapes from the brokenness in this world.

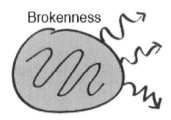

Explain that the pleasures and satisfaction that people get from these things are only temporary, and ultimately lead back to the brokenness. These things aren't all necessarily bad, though. But if you keep chasing these as your purpose or escape, you will always find yourself back in the middle of the brokenness we are trying to escape.

> There is a path before each person that seems right, but it ends in death.
> **Proverbs 14:12**

Hopefully, the picture on the table right now resonates with the friend you are sharing with, as they will have had input on what words are written down. If you're drawing this without hearing their story or including their input, feel free to share about your personal struggles and attempts at escape.

> They traded the truth about God for a lie. So they worshiped and served the things God created instead of the Creator himself, who is worthy of eternal praise! Amen.
> **Romans 1:25**

Brokenness is not a new thing, and people trying to find escapes are not a new thing. This has been happening since the very first man who walked the earth fell into sin. The world is broken because of sin.

> The earth suffers for the sins of its people, for they have twisted God's instructions, violated his laws, and broken his everlasting covenant.
> **Isaiah 24:5**

Week 02, Day 04

Sharing God's Story

Yesterday we talked about circle number one. Today, we will discuss circles two and three. The brokenness that is described and represented by circle number one was never God's desire, nor was it the way He designed things.

Draw a circle in the upper left-hand corner of your canvas. This circle represents God's perfect design, which is love and a relationship with Him. Draw a heart in the middle of the circle to illustrate this.

> Then God said, "Let us make human beings in our image, to be like us. They will reign over the fish in the sea, the birds in the sky, the livestock, all the wild animals on the earth, and the small animals that scurry along the ground." So God created human beings in his own image.

In the image of God he created them; male and female he created them. Then God looked over all he had made, and he saw that it was very good!

Genesis 1:26-27, 31a

In God's perfect design, there was no death, disease, worry, fear, anxiety, or any of the other things that describe brokenness…but mankind was deceived into thinking that they themselves could be like God by sinning. They were told by the devil that sin would lead to a more fulfilling life.

And so they sinned.

Sin is what led us from this perfect world, into a world full of brokenness (draw an arrow from the perfect design circle to the brokenness circle and label it "sin"). And the bad news is, sin is a one-way street. Once you sin, it's too late.

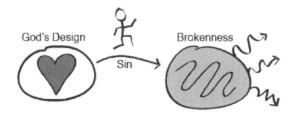

There's no going back to God's perfect design. That's the bad news. But the good news is that when we were unable to get back to God, God decided to come to us!

Draw circle three at the bottom of your canvas, and make it centered. Inside this circle, draw a cross. This represents Jesus, God in the flesh, Who came down to meet us in our brokenness.

> "For this is how God loved the world: He gave his one and only Son, so that everyone who believes in him will not perish but have eternal life."
> **John 3:16**

Jesus was the only person to ever walk this earth while not leaving God's perfect design. He never sinned. He was surrounded by sin, and He was surrounded by brokenness, but Jesus Himself never sinned. And that's important for what comes next.

Jesus lived His life in love, and then He was killed.

He died a brutal death (draw a downward facing arrow to the left of the cross inside the Jesus circle).

But…this was part of God's plan of redemption. You see, God loves us too much to leave us in our brokenness and in our painful attempts at escape. God needed a way to bring us back into His perfect design. But sin is a one-way street, and there is only one way to get sins forgiven.

> For without the shedding of blood,
> there is no forgiveness.
> **Hebrews 9:22**

Because Jesus never sinned, His blood was the perfect payment for the sins of mankind. This is God's plan of redemption!

Because Jesus was God in the flesh, God raised Jesus back to life in order to demonstrate that there was a new hope for mankind. The power of sin had been defeated, and the power of death had been defeated (draw an upward facing arrow to the right of the cross in the Jesus circle)!

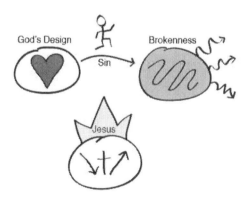

I passed on to you what was most important and what had also been passed on to me. Christ died for our sins, just as the Scriptures said. He was buried, and he was raised from the dead on the third day, just as the Scriptures said.

1 Corinthians 15:3-4

Even though Jesus came down to offer us a way out of the brokenness we are in, and a way back to God's perfect design, it is not an automatic thing. It is something that takes a decision on our part.

There is no judgment against anyone who believes in him. But anyone who does not believe in him has already been judged for not believing in God's one and only Son.

John 3:18

Week 02, Day 05

Connecting the Dots

When Jesus defeated sin and death though His death on the cross, He provided a way back to God's perfect design. Although the world we live in is still broken, there will be a day when God restores His original design in what is called "a new earth."

> Look! I am creating new heavens and a new earth,
> and no one will even think about the old ones anymore.
> **Isaiah 65:17**

Until that time, Jesus made a way for us to have a restored relationship with God through Jesus' death. But in order to be a part of this plan, we have a very real decision to make.

Will we continue to live in this brokenness, chasing escapes? Or will we choose to reject this brokenness and empty escapes, and pursue a full life and true purpose through Jesus instead?

So, how do we move toward the Jesus circle?

There are three things we must do. In order to move from brokenness back into God's design through Jesus (draw an arrow from the brokenness circle to the Jesus circle), we must reject this brokenness and the empty escapes, we must believe in the power of Jesus' death over our sins, and we must follow the way of Jesus.

Instead of "reject," the Bible uses the word "repent." Not only does the word "repent" mean to change directions (stop chasing those escapes as your purpose), but it also means to change your mind (stop believing those escapes will bring you the life that God wants for you in His perfect design). So, reject (or repent from) your old way of living.

> And you will perish, too, unless you repent of your sins and turn to God.
> **Luke 13:3b**

In order to believe, you must simply realize that you are not good enough, and that Jesus *is* good enough! Believe that Jesus truly is Who He says He is (the Son of God), and that His death, burial, and resurrection are enough to cover over your sins.

And then start following Jesus (which is an ongoing effort). Following Jesus simply means to try and do things the way He would do thing, love people the way that He loves people, and think about things the way He would think about things. Instead of being captivated by our escapes, we must allow ourselves to be free in Jesus!

Jesus becomes our King, and He is a good King (draw a crown on the Jesus circle)!

> If you openly declare that Jesus is Lord and believe in your heart that God raised him from the dead, you will be saved. For it is by believing in your heart that you are made right with God, and it is by openly declaring your faith that you are saved.
> **Romans 10:9-10**

And when we start following Jesus, not only do we get to participate in God's perfect design…but we also get to participate in imitating the good nature of Jesus! We get to be good, not because we are trying to escape our brokenness, but because Jesus is good! We're not trying to earn anything!

> God saved you by his grace when you believed. And you can't take credit for this; it is a gift from God. Salvation is not a reward for the good things we have done, so none of us can boast about it.
> **Ephesians 2:8-9**

After we choose to live in the Jesus circle instead of the brokenness circle, Jesus allows us to receive the love of God, and He allows us to grow in a relationship with God Himself (draw an arrow from the Jesus circle to the perfect design circle)!

> This means that anyone who belongs to Christ has become a new person. The old life is gone; a new life has begun! And all of this is a gift from God, who brought us back to himself through Christ. And God has given us this task of reconciling people to him.
> **2 Corinthians 5:17-18**

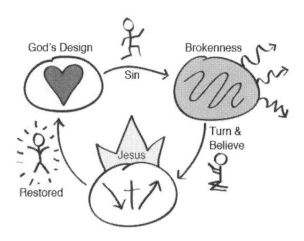

Although this is really good news, I think it gets even better! Not only does Jesus give us an escape from the brokenness and forgiveness of sins...but He also gives us a brand new purpose!

And this brand new purpose is the adventure of a lifetime!

Week 02, Day 06

Your Story in God's Story

It is important that you don't stop there with the "Three Circles" illustration...because the adventure is still ahead of us!

When we find our way back to God's perfect design through the work that Jesus has done for us on the cross, God has a special assignment for us–Go!

> Jesus came and told his disciples, "I have been given all authority in heaven and on earth. Therefore, go and make disciples of all the nations, baptizing them in the name of the Father and the Son and the Holy Spirit. Teach these new disciples to obey all the commands I have given you. And be sure of this: I am with you always, even to the end of the age."
> **Matthew 28:18-20**

After we find our new freedom and healing in Jesus and have access to a restored relationship with God, He wants to send us back out into the brokenness with a purpose to help our friends find the freedom, healing, forgiveness, and purpose that we've found (draw a new dotted line from the God's design circle to the brokenness circle, and label this one "GO")!

Sometimes, people think that the brokenness that they have come out of was too great of a brokenness, and that they are too far gone to ever be used by God. That couldn't be further from the Truth.

Some people think that the escapes that they've pursued were just too bad to ever be forgiven by Jesus. That couldn't be further from the Truth.

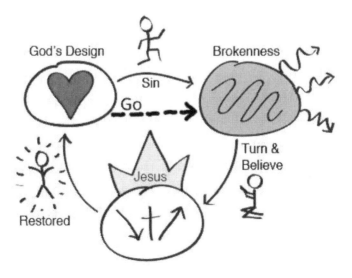

Do you remember back in Week 01, Day 06 when I told you about a terrorist who believed, and was baptized soon after he believed? Well…check out what this same terrorist said later in his life:

> This is a trustworthy saying, and everyone should accept it: "Christ Jesus came into the world to save sinners"— and I am the worst of them all. But God had mercy on me so that Christ Jesus could use me as a prime example of his great patience with even the worst sinners. Then others will realize that they, too, can believe in him and receive eternal life.
> **1 Timothy 1:15-16**

There is nobody too bad or too far gone for Jesus to use.

This is important for you to know as you are sharing the Good News, and it is important for your friend to know as she or he hears the Good News.

After sharing this "Three Circles" illustration with them, be brave. Ask if there is anything stopping them from making this decision to escape their brokenness, and to experience the freedom, healing, forgiveness, and purpose that comes with following Jesus!

If they have questions, encourage them to ask them. If you don't know the answer to their questions, be honest with them and tell them that you don't know, and that you'll try to find the answer for them.

Set a time to meet again, and make sure you come back with the answer to their question (or at least try to). My advice to you is to ask the person you are reading this book with, or maybe a leader in a church that you trust.

If they choose to make the decision to follow Jesus, celebrate with them! You can lead them in a simple prayer that goes something like this:

> "Dear God, I realize that I am broken because of sin, and I am in need of an escape that won't let me down. Thank You for sending Jesus to be the payment for my sins when I was still stuck in my brokenness. I want to choose to start following Jesus today. I believe that He died for my sins, and that He rose again so that I could have freedom, forgiveness, a relationship with You, and a purpose. Help me to stay strong in living my new life with You. In Jesus' name I pray, Amen."

Remember…there are no magic words for making a decision like this, but it is the attitude of their heart. If they sincerely meant that, then praise God with them! Celebrate!

Set a time to meet again soon, and help them start learning what it means to follow Jesus. Maybe you could get them a copy of this book to read through with you?

Whatever you do (whether they choose to follow Jesus or not), do everything you can to remain in relationship with them!

Week 02, Day 07

Some Practical Story Ideas

Knowing how to share the Good News of Jesus does no good if you just keep it to yourself. And yes, it can be intimidating at times to start into a conversation like that…but just remember where you'd be if nobody ever shared with you.

Here is a good Bible verse to remember:

> For "Everyone who calls on the name of the Lord will be saved." But how can they call on him to save them unless they believe in him? And how can they believe in him if they have never heard about him? And how can they hear about him unless someone tells them? And how will anyone go and tell them without being sent? That is why the Scriptures say, "How beautiful are the feet of messengers who bring good news!"
> **Romans 10:13-15**

Today I want to give you some super practical ideas on how you can begin a natural, non-threatening, and non-intimidating conversation about Jesus with one of your friends, or maybe even a stranger.

1. Ask "What's the best thing that ever happened to you?"

People love to share about the time that they got super lucky and won something big, or when they found the love of their life, or when something else good and big happened to them! So, ask! But be sure you are ready to listen. There's nothing worse than when somebody asks you a question, and you get excited about sharing your answer, only to realize that they are not really that interested in what you have to say. So, listen well!

2. Do a service project together.

One really cool way to build trust with somebody and get into deep conversations with them is to serve side by side. Find a local charity or nonprofit that is doing some really good work in your community, and ask them if they'd like to volunteer with you!

While you are volunteering together, make sure to be intentional about getting to know them better. Ask them good questions, and listen well. When they ask questions back, give thoughtful answers.

One thing that is important to keep in mind is to be reciprocal with your answers. If they ask, "How are you?," don't reply with a simple "Good." That ends the conversation right there and makes them feel awkward! Instead say, "Good, how are you?" That way, it keeps the conversation alive.

3. Make a list of friends you'd like to share with, and start praying for them.

This one seems really simple, but honestly…it works. Begin praying for opportunities to share with some of your friends, and you'll be surprised at the opportunities that God sends your way!

Remember that the Holy Spirit is living inside of you, and that the Holy Spirit has a desire to draw people to Jesus. The Holy Spirit wants people to know about Jesus more than you do! So start praying, and see what happens!

4. Be intentional in your "third places."

People typically have their "first place," and that is where they live (and probably spend the majority of their time). Then, they also have their "second place," and that's where they work or go to school.

But when they want to do something fun while relaxing, a lot of people have a "third place." Usually, these are places where people gather, and some people are considered "regulars." Coffee shops, bars, restaurants, bowling alleys, hobby shops…you get the idea!

When you are in one of your "third places," be prayerful about who is around you. Look around with curious eyes. Listen to the conversations that are happening around you. Ask the barista how their day is going. Be prayerfully attentive to those who are around you, and before you know it, there may be an opportunity to share the Good News with somebody in a natural way!

5. Always be ready!

You never know when an opportunity will arise, especially if you're praying for one!

> And if someone asks about your hope as a believer, always be ready to explain it.
> **1 Peter 3:15b**

I am praying for you as you work towards this!

Week 03

Talking to God

A lot of believers are intimidated by the idea of praying, *especially* praying out loud in front of other people. And while we are never commanded to pray out loud in public, we are definitely told by Jesus that we, as Christians, need to be praying people.

> One day Jesus told his disciples a story to show that they should always pray and never give up.
> **Luke 18:1**

But praying really isn't as hard as it sounds. It literally is just talking to God. If you know how to talk to someone you love (and who loves you back), then you are well on your way to knowing how to pray! But even though it's a simple thing to do, there are still some proper ways to pray. Hopefully, today's reading will help you have a more robust prayer life!

Don't worry about anything; instead, pray about everything. Tell God what you need, and thank him for all he has done. Then you will experience God's peace, which exceeds anything we can understand. His peace will guard your hearts and minds as you live in Christ Jesus.
Philippians 4:6–7

Whenever we begin to worry or feel anxious, God encourages us to pray. Just like a caring parent who comforts their child during times of anxiety, God, our heavenly Father, wants us to be free from worry. As we learned from the Philippians verse we just read, prayer is our way to find peace and comfort, just as a child finds solace in their parent's embrace. So when we pray, we should pray:

1. For our needs

If an anxious child came up to their loving parents with a need, there is absolutely no doubt in my mind that a loving parent would do whatever is best for their child.

Give all your worries and cares to God, for he cares about you.
1 Peter 5:7

2. To give thanks/praise to God

Besides the fact that saying "thank you" is a nice thing to do, it is something we are commanded to do. And when we thank God for all that He has done, I honestly believe that it affects our attitude and our outlook on life.

When we focus on the good things that God has done, we are more likely to do good things for others who are in need around us! And that's never a bad thing.

> Therefore, let us offer through Jesus a continual sacrifice of praise to God, proclaiming our allegiance to his name. And don't forget to do good and to share with those in need. These are the sacrifices that please God.
> **Hebrews 13:15-16**

3. To experience God's peace

God's peace is a peace "which exceeds anything we can understand." And not only is it a greater peace than we can understand, but His peace guards our hearts and our minds. When we pray, we can experience this peace! The peace that comes with knowing that our sins are forgiven, and that comes with knowing that Jesus did everything needed for our salvation!

In addition to those things, we can also pray to God for:

1. Wisdom & Guidance

How many times are you faced with a difficult decision of where to go, or what to do with your life? Maybe it's a job situation, or a housing difficulty, or a relationship choice…well now you don't have to make those decisions alone! God promises us that if we will pray to Him for wisdom, He will give it to us.

But it's not automatic. In order to receive the wisdom, we've got to believe He will give it to us, and listen for it. God can speak to us in a variety of different ways. We'll talk more about God talking to us in just two days, and I'll tell you several different ways we can listen to God's voice in our lives. But for now, check out this verse about the promise we have that God will grant us wisdom when we truly seek it from Him:

> If you need wisdom, ask our generous God, and he will give it to you. He will not rebuke you for asking. But when you ask him, be sure that your faith is in God alone. Do not waver, for a person with divided loyalty is as unsettled as a wave of the sea that is blown and tossed by the wind.
> **James 1:5-6**

2. Forgiveness

Even though we have the Spirit of God in us, and even though we may be filled with the Spirit on a daily basis…we will still fall into sin often. It's that pesky "civil war" thing I talked about in Week 01, Day 03. When we do fall into sin, God promises that He will forgive us over and over when we come to Him and seek forgiveness. God does not want us to live our lives in guilt.

> Have mercy on me, O God,
>   because of your unfailing love.
> Because of your great compassion,
>   blot out the stain of my sins.
> **Psalm 51:1**

3. For God to bless others

As we grow in our faith, we will find ourselves praying for others more and more. Maybe it's somebody who is sick, or who is going through a really hard time…there is power in praying for others. We can pray for others to be blessed or healed when they are sick, suffering, or otherwise grieving.

Check out this verse about praying for others:

Are any of you suffering hardships? You should pray. Are any of you happy? You should sing praises. Are any of you sick? You should call for the elders of the church to come and pray over you, anointing you with oil in the name of the Lord. Such a prayer offered in faith will heal the sick, and the Lord will make you well. And if you have committed any sins, you will be forgiven. Confess your sins to each other and pray for each other so that you may be healed. The earnest prayer of a righteous person has great power and produces wonderful results.
James 5:13-16

And finally, we should pray often. There's a verse that sums up how often we should be praying:

Never stop praying.
1 Thessalonians 5:17

That's pretty strait forward. There's not a whole bunch   of ways to interpret this verse other than…we should pray all the time. Pray while you're walking, driving, eating, reading, and whatever else you do and wherever else you do it…pray!

Week 03, Day 02

Talking to God, Part 2

When you are talking to God, there are many different "types" of prayers you can say. Of course, many people tend to "mix and match" prayer types, instead of simply sticking to one subject (much like the conversations you have with the people you love). When you talk to God, you want it to be more like conversations with somebody Who truly loves you, instead of making them "transactional" conversations (where you're just trying to get something).

Here are examples of different types of prayers:

1. Prayers of Praise

This is pretty self-explanatory. Just tell God how good He is! Tell Him some things that you like about Him! Or, tell Him about some of the things He has done that you really appreciate. Things like…creating you!

> Thank you for making me so wonderfully complex! Your workmanship is marvelous—how well I know it.
> **Psalm 139:14**

Just think of some things that you are really grateful for about God, and pray those words to Him. It doesn't have to be any more complicated than that!

2. Prayers of Thankfulness

This is different than praise because it is more focused on things He has done that you (or we) do not deserve. "Thank You for forgiving me," or something like "Thank You for this opportunity You sent my way." What has God done for you recently? Are there any problems you've asked Him for help with that you have seen resolved? If you're having trouble coming up with something to thank Him for, simply thank Him for His love for us! Simply tell Him how grateful you are for Him!

> Give thanks to the Lord, for he is good!
> His faithful love endures forever.
> **1 Chronicles 16:34**

3. Prayer Requests

I've mentioned before (*Curious?* book, Week 07, Day 05), but Jesus isn't your genie in a bottle. He is not a vending machine. He is not somebody who is there to grant your every wish and whim…but He does love you, and He does want to provide for you. Therefore, we are encouraged to approach God with our needs, wants, and concerns. Listen to what Jesus Himself said about praying like this:

> That is why I tell you not to worry about everyday life—whether you have enough food and drink, or enough clothes to wear. Isn't life more than food, and your body more than clothing?…Seek the Kingdom of God above all else, and live righteously, and he will give you everything you need.
>
> **Matthew 6:25, 33**

4. Prayers of Confession

There are going to be times that you mess up. Even though the Holy Spirit is with you, and even though you are following Jesus…sin is something that we will continue to be plagued with until the day that we are able to be face to face with Jesus in heaven. That's one of the symptoms of "the flesh" we are in.

> But if we confess our sins to him, he is faithful and just to forgive us our sins and to cleanse us from all wickedness.
> **1 John 1:9**

When you mess up (and you will), don't beat yourself up too much about it. Ask God to forgive you, and do your best to do better next time. God will forgive you.

5. Prayers for Help for Others (Intercession)

People you know are going to go through some hard times. Maybe they'll experience sickness, or financial hardship, or relationship problems. As Christians, we are called to help them when we can, but we are also encouraged to pray for them.

> I urge you, first of all, to pray for all people. Ask God to help them; intercede on their behalf, and give thanks for them.
> **1 Timothy 2:1**

I've found it helpful to pray for somebody on the spot if they ask me to pray for them. Because, if you're anything like me, you'll say "Yeah, I'll pray for you!" and then completely forget to actually pray later on. Sometimes, in order to keep your word, it is most helpful to pray for your friend in the moment. Not only does that help you stay honest, but it is a powerful thing!

So, we've just explored five different types of prayers we can pray. Like I said, sometimes it is helpful to mix and match prayers subjects, much like a normal conversation with somebody you love and who loves you back!

Here's the big idea: Talk to God throughout your day, and do your best to listen to what He is telling you as well (more on this at the end of this week).

Sometimes, when I'm not sure how to pray, I follow this model:

A - Adoration (Praise)
C - Confession
T - Thankfulness
S - Supplication (Requests & Intercession)

Why don't you try praying this model today?

Tell God how you adore Him, how you've failed Him, thank Him for being faithful to forgive you, and ask Him to meet the needs in your life.

Week 03, Day 03

Talking to God, Part 3

When you're talking to God, here are some tips to make your prayers more powerful and effective:

1. When you pray, pray in Jesus' name

> You can ask for anything in my name, and I will do it, so that the Son can bring glory to the Father.
> **John 14:23**

Now, this is a commonly misunderstood verse, and a commonly misunderstood concept. Just because you say "In Jesus' name I pray" at the end of your prayer does not for one second mean that everything in your prayer is going to come true. You may be thinking, "yeah but that Bible verse says I can ask for anything!" True…but it also says "in my name," being, the name of Jesus.

When you pray in the name of Jesus, it means praying according to His will. It means praying according to His purposes, and in His Spirit.

Remember back when we were talking about being filled with the Spirit? It's similar to that. Praying in Jesus' name while being filled with His Spirit. Praying for things in His name mean praying in alignment to His will. This verse explains it a little bit better:

> And we are confident that he hears us whenever we ask for anything that pleases him. And since we know he hears us when we make our requests, we also know that he will give us what we ask for.
> **1 John 5:14-15**

2. Sometimes, pray with your eyes open

A good example of when you should pray with your eyes open? Well…when you're driving!

When I was growing up, I thought that it was disrespectful to God to pray with your eyes open. That couldn't be further from the truth. People started closing their eyes when they prayed to tune out other distractions, and sometimes it's good to do the same. But honestly, God would rather us pray more often than to only pray when we are in a place where we can safely (and naturally) close our eyes.

What about while you're in the grocery store? Chances are, people might look at you a little weird if you stop in the middle of the cereal section to close your eyes and pray. But, God would rather you pray in the cereal section with your eyes open than to forego praying.

Pray often, especially in places that seem unlikely!

3. Don't be weird when you pray

Have you ever noticed that when some people pray, they all of the sudden sound like they're talking like a pirate? Or like they're gasping for air?

I'm not saying you need to make fun of how anybody prays (you shouldn't), but at the same time, I think God is most glorified when we pray in a natural way, as a child talking to their Father who truly loves them.

We should be respectful when we pray, yes. But we shouldn't use unnecessarily large words, or any accents that we don't use in real life. Honestly, that sometimes does nothing more than draw attention to ourselves. And if the attention is on us during group prayer instead of on God, then I think we need to change things up just a little bit.

Nothing that we do should draw attention to ourselves over attention to God.

> When you pray, don't babble on and on as the Gentiles do. They think their prayers are answered merely by repeating their words again and again.
> **Matthew 6:7**

To end our section on prayer, I want to explore what Jesus gave His followers as the "model prayer." This is what Jesus said when His disciples asked Him how they should pray:

> Pray like this:
> Our Father in heaven, may your name be kept holy. May your Kingdom come soon. May your will be done on earth, as it is in heaven. Give us today the food we need, and forgive us our sins, as we have forgiven those who sin against us. And don't let us yield to temptation, but rescue us from the evil one.
> **Matthew 6:9-13**

In this one prayer, we see several things modeled:

1. Talking to God like He is a loving Father
2. Praising God for Who He is
3. Praying for the world to be set right (and in doing this, Jesus may reveal to us what He wants us to do to help)!
4. Praying that the Kingdom of God would be revealed on earth (this is what happens when the hungry get fed, and the strangers are welcomed in as family, etc)
5. Asking God to keep leading us in the way He wants us to go
6. Mentioning prayer requests, and also interceding for others
7. Admitting to God the ways that we have fallen short
8. Praying that God would keep us strong against the enemy's schemes and the temptations of the flesh that try to make you fall into sin.

I'm not sure what your thoughts are on that…but wow! What a powerful prayer!

I challenge you to try praying similar prayers this week.

Share how your prayer life changes when you pray like this with the friend you're reading this book with!

Week 03, Day 04

God Talking to Us

There are many ways that God can speak to us: through other believers (**2 Samuel 12**), through circumstances (**Acts 17:26-29**), through dreams (**Matthew 2:19-20**), and in many other ways. But what's the primary way that God has spoken to people across time and geography, and continues to speak to people today?

Through His Word, the Bible.

Because God's Word is the primary way that God speaks to us, we must learn to consume it, not just simply read it. We should learn to understand it, grow in it, share it, and allow it to change our lives to make us look more like Jesus.

> Oh, the joys of those who do not follow the advice of the wicked, or stand around with sinners, or join in with

mockers. But they delight in the law of the Lord, meditating on it day and night. They are like trees planted along the riverbank, bearing fruit each season. Their leaves never wither, and they prosper in all they do.

Psalm 1:1-3

Reading the Bible (listening to what God is saying) is a vital part of the Christian life. But the Bible should also be read differently than a typical book. There are many different effective ways to read and study the Bible, but I'm going to introduce you to one that is really easy and effective.

1. Read a passage

It's always good to start by actually reading what you are studying! But I added the words "a passage" specifically because I think it's important to read a certain predetermined portion when studying. It could be a single verse, or a complete thought, or a paragraph, or longer. I recommend starting with a complete thought, and adjusting accordingly after you get the hang of this method I'm going to tell you about.

2. Write the passage

The next step is to grab a notebook or piece of paper (or phone), and write the particular passage word for word, being intentional to think about each and every word as you are writing it. Doing this will cause you to think about each individual word, and may even change the way you see the verse.

During this step, it's helpful to read the passage out loud. This is an important step and should not be skipped, *especially* for a passage that might be familiar. This step might even help you see a verse you may have read hundreds of times over in an entirely different light.

Another helpful thing during this step might be listening to Scripture being read by a Bible app, or another person if you're doing this in a group. Listen to it slowly. Listen to it multiple times.

3. Write the passage in your own words

Be sure not to change the meaning of anything you don't like or are uncomfortable with, but write the passage in your own words. Think about each word and phrase intentionally, and then write it out as if you were telling it to a friend. Use your own words to do this (no need to make it sound super fancy).

Writing it down in your own words makes you think about the meaning of each and every word even more. If you'd rather, you can use a voice recording app to record yourself explaining the verse in your own words instead. Make sure it doesn't lose the meaning of the original Scripture, though. And make sure that it is done in your own words, as if you were talking to a friend.

Don't move on to the next step until you've got this communicated in your own words, and would even be able to communicate the idea to somebody else. One sign of true understanding is that you are able to explain it to somebody else. If you have questions about certain things in the passage, feel free to ask a mentor, or a leader within the church that you are attending.

You'll find that on longer passages, or passages that are more difficult to understand, this step may take more than one day. That's ok. You're not in a huge rush.

True understanding and transformation is way more important than the speed at which you can skim over information.

And remember this: We don't study the Bible for information. We study the Bible for transformation.

We study the Bible for life change.

It's hard to truly obey something that you do not fully understand.

Week 03, Day 05

God Talking to Us, Part 2

After you finish reading the passage, writing it word for word, and sharing it in your own words, then it's time for a commitment.

4. Make a commitment(s)

Instead of just talking about it, now we transition to making commitments to do something about it. Pray through the passage, and read it several more times in both the Bible and the version that you wrote out.

What does Jesus desire from us?

Here are some helpful questions you can ask during this section:

- What really stands out to me?
- What is my favorite thing about this passage?

- Is there something that bothers me about this passage?
- What is this passage telling me about God?
- What is this passage telling me about mankind?
- What is this passage telling me about me?
- Is there a behavior I should copy?
- Are there any instructions I should obey?
- Is there something I should stop doing?
- Is there something I can lean on for hope?
- Who in my life should I share this with?
- What questions do I have about this passage?

After you think through these questions, or questions similar to these, make a list of things you are committing to do. Remember that the Bible is not just a window you should use to view the world around you, but it is also a mirror that you should use to examine yourself.

> But don't just listen to God's word. You must do what it says. Otherwise, you are only fooling yourselves. For if you listen to the word and don't obey, it is like glancing at your face in a mirror. You see yourself, walk away, and forget what you look like. But if you look carefully into the perfect law that sets you free, and if you do what it says and don't forget what you heard, then God will bless you for doing it.
> **James 1:22-25**

And don't forget to write down your questions. Ask a mentor if she or he has the answer, or maybe just discuss the question with a friend.

When I was several years younger, there was a pastor who told me, "If you ask questions about the Bible, that shows God that your faith is weak and that you are doubting Him." To be clear, that cannot be further from the truth. God is pleased when we meditate (think on) His Words, and when we seek answers to the things we do not fully understand.

5. Pray

Very simply, this should not be a one-way conversation. Pray at the beginning, pray at the end, and pray in the middle. Talk to God as He is talking to you!

6. Share

When you learn new things from God's Word, He is pleased when we don't just keep it to ourselves, but share it with others around us! Now, I'm not talking about telling them how they should change their lives…that's not your place. Instead, tell them how you are changing your life! And when you are open, honest, and vulnerable with others about what God is teaching you and what He is doing in your life, it will inspire similar changes in theirs.

7. Do it again!

And keep doing it!

Now that you know this extremely simple but effective way of studying the Bible, why don't you do it right now? In fact, why don't you try practicing on this verse that may be familiar to you:

> For this is how God loved the world: He gave his one and only Son, so that everyone who believes in him will not perish but have eternal life.
> **John 3:16**

You might be surprised at how hard it is to write something familiar in your own words. Or, you might be surprised at a new realization you have in step two!

Don't rush it! Take your time!

Week 03, Day 06

Private Conversations with God

We've discussed that prayer is talking to God, and that the primary method God uses to talk to us is through Scripture reading. When you use these two things together, you can have conversations with God.

Sometimes you might hear some people call these conversations "quiet times," and others may call them "devotions." Regardless of what you call them, they are important. And in every healthy conversation, there is both talking and listening. And just like in healthy, loving relationships…these conversations should happen regularly (hopefully, daily).

Not only do we need to spend time together one-on-one with God in order to get to know Him better, but it is also such a privilege to be able to have a private audience with the Creator of the universe!

When we spend time with God in this way, not only is it honoring to Him, but we are also following the example of Jesus:

> Before daybreak the next morning, Jesus got up and went out to an isolated place to pray.
> **Mark 1:35**

Every conversation that we have with God should have at least three purposes:

1. For us to worship God.
2. For our relationship with God to grow deeper.
3. For us to be led by God's will.

This really is simple, but these conversations are far too often overlooked by everyday believers. But when we see a great movement of God happening in our world, there is usually a woman or man behind that movement who is serious about their private conversations with God.

In order to consistently have strong conversations with God, I find that most people do well to have some sort of consistent pattern and plan. While each person is different, here are a few tools that I recommend you at least start with (and once you get the hang of it, adjust as needed):

1. A Bible

While other devotional books are fine, they should never take the place of your Bible. Your Bible is God's Words directly to you, and is in His own voice. A devotional is written by a woman or man who is interpreting God's Words through their own voice… always go directly to the source whenever possible!

There are many different translations available, and there are hundreds of opinions on which one you should get, and which one is best, etc. Here's the bottom line when it comes to translations: What works best for you? What's the easiest for you to understand? What's the easiest for you to read every day?

Some people, genuinely prefer the "King James Version" (KJV), and use it every day. That's the one that sounds to me like pirate talk… "thou" instead of "you," "hast" instead of "have," and a bunch of words that are too big (or old) for me to understand.

In case you're wondering, the translation used in this book is called the "New Living Translation" (NLT), and it is my preference. It's easy for me to understand, it's easy for me to read regardless of what time of day it is (even if I'm tired), and it's easy for me to share with others for them to understand as well.

2. A notebook

Call it a journal, a diary, or simply "Bible study notes"…it really doesn't matter. What's important is to have somewhere to write down what God is telling you as He speaks to you through His Word. It's also cool to be able to write down what you're praying for, and how you see God moving through your prayers and/or life in general.

3. A plan

When are you going to do this? First thing in the morning (like Jesus did)? At night before you go to sleep? Regardless of when, it's good to have a consistent time/pattern.

How long are you going to spend doing this each day? Five minutes? Half an hour? Keep in mind that it's better to spend a few minutes alone with God than to not spend any time at all.

Where are you going to do this? Will you have a dedicated space? Will you be secluded in a room by yourself? Surrounded by people at the coffee shop with background noise? While some people need absolute silence and solitude in order to concentrate well and hear from God, there are other people with a certain… let's call it a "disorder," who actually do better surrounded by people and background noise (I literally have an app on my phone that plays "coffee shop chatter" for when my ADHD can't handle the silence). What works better for you? The answer to that question is what you should do.

Finally, what are you going to study? I mean…the Bible, yeah. But the Bible is a really big book! What, specifically, are you going to read? Are you going to read topical passages (verses on anger, or joy, or life in the church, etc.), or are you going to read straight through different books of the Bible?

My recommendation is to do the latter. Read through books of the Bible, and allow God to speak to you through the Bible as it was meant to be read.

Are you going to try and read the Bible through in a year? Or, are you going to take your time and aim for understanding instead of simply consumption? Quality over quantity?

This is what I recommend…take your time.

We'll talk about this later (in Week 05), but God doesn't want us to stop at simply filling our head with knowledge (which can happen when you focus on reading things too quickly). He also wants His Word to affect our hearts (how we love) and our hands (what we do).

When you put all those things into place, you will begin to have conversations with God that are truly life-giving. And remember…conversations go two ways. Let Him speak to you.

While letting God speak to you, sometimes intentional questions help while you are reading Scripture. When you have time, revisit Week 03, Day 05 for a good list of questions to ask yourself while reading through Scripture.

Listen to what Jesus said about the importance of maintaining a personal and consistent relationship with God:

> Seek the Kingdom of God above all else, and live righteously, and he will give you everything you need.
> **Matthew 6:33**

And remember…the Kingdom of God is not just about getting you to heaven when you leave this earth someday, it's about getting heaven to earth today.

God has given you a unique design, a unique calling, and unique gifts to help you do just that. More on that later (Week 07).

But for now, let's get into regular conversation with God!

Week 03, Day 07

Group Conversations with God

While it is vital to have private conversations with God, it is also beneficial to have group conversations with God sometimes! Usually, these are called "Group Bible Studies," "Small Group," or maybe even something like a "Missional Community." A good size for groups like this is typically four to twelve individuals, so that everybody has a chance to share.

Just like when you have group conversations in your everyday life, a group Bible study should give the opportunity for each individual to connect with each other, for each individual to talk to God, and for each individual to hear from God.

Everybody is encouraged to talk, and everybody listens. Some weeks will be easier to do this than others, but remember that it is always better to focus on relationships over the rules.

There are multiple formats or group study guidelines that you could follow to make things consistent and fruitful, but I'm going to focus on one called "Discovery Bible Study."

1. Talk

In this format, each individual present is encouraged to start by reflecting on their week or month. Go around the group and ask intentional questions like:

> How was your week (or month)?
> What are you celebrating?
> What are you struggling with?
> Is there a need within our community?
> Is there something we can do to help?

2. Pray

Now that everybody has caught up, pray. Be sure to include elements of what you heard during this prayer. How you pray is totally up to the leader or the group.

One person can be designated for prayer, or if everybody is comfortable with it, you can go around the room and allow each individual a chance to pray.

3. Recall & Reflect

This step can be skipped for the very first meeting, but for the second meeting and beyond, it should never be skipped. It is important to remember what God is telling us from meeting to meeting, and to reflect on how we might have even changed.

Have somebody share/retell the story from the last group Bible study meeting, and allow time for the group to reflect.
During this section, it is helpful to ask questions like:

> Did this story result in a life change?
> Did this story result in a behavior change?
> Were you able to share this story with someone else?

4. Read & Retell

Have somebody read the designated passage for the day. Make sure that this individual reads it out loud, and not too quickly. The goal of this section is not to get through the passage as quickly as you can, but for everybody to better understand what the passage is actually saying.

After the passage is complete, have somebody volunteer to retell the story or the passage from memory. They are going to miss some things, that's only natural. Let them tell the story, and let them finish. And after they are finished retelling the story, then open it up to the rest of the group to fill in the blanks of what was missed.

This step should not be considered complete until the entire group agrees that they have successfully retold the story, and filled in all the missing pieces. Feel free to revisit the passage in Scripture if any serious questions arise about what is correct.

5. Read & First Look

As a group, read the passage again. But during this "first look" section, you want to focus on answering these questions:

> What does this passage tell us about God?
> What does this passage tell us about Jesus?
> What does this passage tell us about God's master plan?

6. Read & Second Look

Read the passage again, but this time focus on these questions:

> What does this passage tell us about mankind?
> What does this passage tell us about the world?

7. Internalize It

In this section, we should resist the temptation to focus on what somebody else should do because of this passage. Instead, we need to focus on what needs to happen in our own life. Think about what needs to change in you. How should your life look different than it looks today? Ask questions like:

What does this passage indicate I am doing well?
What does this passage indicate I need to change?

8. Share & Grow

After we have internalized the passage is when we can begin to think about others in our lives that might need to hear it. But, when sharing with others, be very careful not to fall into the trap of being "judgey." Sometimes, especially with people who are not close to God, it is better to share of God's love than of God's wrath (although both are important). During this section ask questions like this:

Who do I know that needs to hear this?
How and when can I share with them?
Is there somebody I should invite to this group?
Is it time to start a new group?

Follow these steps, and you will have completed a "Discovery Bible Study." I recommend getting to know the "rhythm" of the group and the guidelines before making any major changes. But, after you get to know the people and the process, by all means customize it to make it fit the group better!

Here are some tips I've found to be helpful:

> Try to be sure everybody gets a chance to share.
> Focus on the passage at hand, not other passages.
> Silence is your friend (people are thinking).
> The leader should simply facilitate, not teach.
> Start and end on time (informal hangout after is ok).
> Make sure you get to each section each time.
> It is ok to skip specific questions for time's sake.
> Read the passage before the group meeting.
> Pray over the passage before the group meeting.
> Send out the passage you'll be reading in advance.

When questions arise, I've found these responses to be helpful and thought provoking:

> "How does the passage answer that question?"
> "Where is that idea found in this passage?"
> "Can you rephrase that question? Help us understand it?"

Week 04

God the Father

There are many different ways that God reveals Himself to us in the Bible, but there are three primary manifestations that we are going to focus on this week: God the Father, God the Son, and God the Holy Spirit - this is referred to as "the Holy Trinity."

Now, I realize even though some people have fantastic relationships with their earthly/biological fathers, that is not the case for the majority of people I know. Fathers, it seems, have a reputation for being absent, abusive, or apathetic. If one of these words describes your father, then please keep reading…because God is way, way better!

If you remember back to Day 03 of last week, Jesus taught us to pray to God as if He is our Father. And today and tomorrow, my aim is to show you why He is a good, good Father!

1. Our Heavenly Father's Unconditional Love

I know that when some people say stuff about the love of our Heavenly Father, that may not mean anything positive to many people who have had abusive fathers here on earth. But…God's love is so much different! God's love for us, as His children, is unconditional! That means nothing we do can make Him love us less…and nothing we do can make Him love us more!

Even though we are sinners, and even though God absolutely hates sin, check out this verse about God the Father's great love:

> But God showed his great love for us by sending Christ to die for us while we were still sinners.
> **Romans 5:8**

Not only is God's great love demonstrated by the death of His one and only Son, but it is also demonstrated by not letting His one and only Son stay dead!

> But God is so rich in mercy, and he loved us so much, that even though we were dead because of our sins, he gave us life when he raised Christ from the dead. (It is only by God's grace that you have been saved!)
> **Ephesians 2:4-5**

One of my favorite stories about God's unconditional love for us is found in one of the stories (also called "parables") that Jesus told the people around Him while He was here on earth in **Luke 15:11-32**. This story is most commonly known as "The Parable of the Prodigal Son." It is too long for me to print here, but when you have the chance, you should check out this story that Jesus told to the group of "notorious sinners" that were gathered around Him!

Jesus was extremely intentional about telling those around Him of the Father's great and unconditional love for them…and His great and unconditional love for us!

2. Our Heavenly Father's Protection

Just like a loving father will keep his children from things that will harm them, our Heavenly Father will guard our souls from the evil one (the devil). In fact, check out this verse that basically says exactly that:

> But the Lord is faithful; he will strengthen you and guard you from the evil one.
> **2 Thessalonians 3:3**

That's a good one to keep tucked away for when times get hard!

Not only will our Heavenly Father guard our souls from the enemy, but He will even be there to help us when the temptation to sin becomes unbearable.

> The temptations in your life are no different from what others experience. And God is faithful. He will not allow the temptation to be more than you can stand. When you are tempted, he will show you a way out so that you can endure.
> **1 Corinthians 10:13**

But just because God will show us a way out, doesn't mean we will take it. We are still our own persons, and much like children…sometimes we make stupid decisions. But when we do something dumb, we need to be sure to never blame God.

> And remember, when you are being tempted, do not say, "God is tempting me." God is never tempted to do wrong, and he never tempts anyone else. Temptation comes from our own desires, which entice us and drag us away.
> **James 1:13-14**

I can tell you there are times I do something to protect my children, but they still get hurt from their own choices. But when hurt comes, we should not blame God.

Week 04, Day 02

God the Father, Part 2

Yesterday, we covered two distinct reasons why God is a great Father to His children (unlike some of our fathers here on earth who sometimes tend to miss the mark). Today, I'm excited to share with you some more reasons why and how God is a good, good Father!

3. Our Heavenly Father's Provisions

Not only does our Heavenly Father protect us, but He provides for us as well! One Bible verse that I've always particularly liked about how God provides for us is this one:

> You parents—if your children ask for a loaf of bread, do you give them a stone instead? Or if they ask for a fish, do you give them a snake? Of course not! So if you sinful

people know how to give good gifts to your children, how much more will your heavenly Father give good gifts to those who ask him.

Matthew 7:9-11

When we are in need, our Heavenly Father will meet our needs! Now, that is much different than saying He will meet all of our "wants" (I'd sure like to win the lottery, but our Heavenly Father has not given that to me…but He is still so good)!

And this same God who takes care of me will supply all your needs from his glorious riches, which have been given to us in Christ Jesus.

Philippians 4:19

Our good, good Father takes joy in providing for our needs!

4. Our Heavenly Father's Loving Discipline

This one is not as fun to read about as the other ones, but this is an indication of God's true love for us. When a parent truly loves their kids, there will be some sort of discipline involved in order to help them learn the right way.

Now let me hit pause right here and be very clear about this: discipline and abuse are NOT the same thing. In fact, Jesus

Himself had some pretty harsh words for anybody who would harm a child. Listen to these words from Jesus:

> But if you cause one of these little ones who trusts in me to fall into sin, it would be better for you to have a large millstone tied around your neck and be drowned in the depths of the sea.
> **Matthew 18:6**

There is never an acceptable time for abuse, or for causing a child to fall into sin. But there are plenty of acceptable times for loving discipline. For instance, if my son decides that he likes playing "house" in the oven while it is off...I will discipline him. Especially if he keeps doing it, you better believe I will lovingly chastise him, ground him, and maybe even spank him. Is this because I don't love him?

Not at all. In fact, it's the opposite.

I would lovingly discipline him in this scenario because I know something that he does not know...that he can get *severely* hurt, or even accidentally killed if he continues that behavior. My discipline is a result of my love, and that is how God lovingly chooses to deal with us.

And have you forgotten the encouraging words God spoke to you as his children? He said, "My child, don't make light of the Lord's discipline, and don't give up when he corrects you. For the Lord disciplines those he loves, and he punishes each one he accepts as his child."

As you endure this divine discipline, remember that God is treating you as his own children. Who ever heard of a child who is never disciplined by its father? If God doesn't discipline you as he does all of his children, it means that you are illegitimate and are not really his children at all.

Hebrews 12:5-8

God's incredible, unconditional, undying love for us is demonstrated in these ways. And God is a Father who is worth trusting, embracing, and loving back. He will never disappoint!

So if you have (or had) an amazing father figure here on earth, just imagine…God is even better! But if you had a poor (or absent) example of a father figure here on earth, trust that God is able to redeem even the most painful of experiences.

God is a good, good Father!

Week 04, Day 03

God the Son

In the Holy Trinity (the Father, the Son, and the Holy Spirit), Jesus is identified as God the Son, or the Son of God. It's important to note that this is not because God got married and had kids...but because God, in His perfect plan of redemption and reconciliation with mankind that had fallen into sin, decided that the best way for Him to relate to mankind was to become human.

> In the beginning the Word already existed. The Word was with God, and the Word was God.
>
> So the Word became human and made his home among us. He was full of unfailing love and faithfulness. And we have seen his glory, the glory of the Father's one and only Son.
> **John 1:1, 14**

God Himself became flesh so that He could not only relate with our struggles, but so that He could pay the price that He Himself demanded for the forgiveness of our sins.

> For without the shedding of blood,
> there is no forgiveness.
> **Hebrews 9:22b**

The following verse describing the process of Jesus becoming human actually includes all three People of the Trinity contained within a single verse. Check out what the angel of the Lord said to Mary (the human mother of Jesus):

> The angel replied, "The Holy Spirit will come upon you, and the power of the Most High will overshadow you. So the baby to be born will be holy, and he will be called the Son of God.
> **Luke 1:35**

God the Holy Spirit was with Mary while the power of the Most High (God the Father) overshadowed her, and she became pregnant with Jesus (God the Son).

Jesus' mother was Mary (human), but Jesus' Father is God (God the Father).

This is important because in order for the sins of mankind to be forever paid for, there had to be a blood sacrifice from a man. And for the blood of a man to pay for the sins of somebody else, that person had to be sinless. Every single human who is conceived by the seed of another man inherits sin. So, in order for Jesus to be both human *and* sinless, He had to have a human mother, but a non-human Father.

> When Adam sinned, sin entered the world. Adam's sin brought death, so death spread to everyone, for everyone sinned.
>
> Yes, Adam's one sin brings condemnation for everyone, but Christ's one act of righteousness brings a right relationship with God and new life for everyone. Because one person disobeyed God, many became sinners. But because one other person obeyed God, many will be made righteous.
> **Romans 5:12, 18-19**

Jesus identified Himself as the Son of God while He walked this earth. It was no secret that this meant that He was also God Himself. One of the easy ways to see this is to look at when Jesus was being tried before the religious elite of His day, and the Jewish rulers. The charge that got Jesus sentenced to death was blasphemy: Claiming to be God, or claiming to be equal to God.

But Jesus remained silent. Then the high priest said to him, "I demand in the name of the living God—tell us if you are the Messiah, the Son of God."

Jesus replied, "You have said it. And in the future you will see the Son of Man seated in the place of power at God's right hand and coming on the clouds of heaven."

Then the high priest tore his clothing to show his horror and said, "Blasphemy! Why do we need other witnesses? You have all heard his blasphemy. What is your verdict?" "Guilty!" they shouted. "He deserves to die!"
Matthew 26:63-66

God the Father loved the mankind He created so much that He came down in the form of God the Son (Jesus) in order to die for our sins, so that we wouldn't have to die for our own sins.

Because of the death of God the Son, we have access to a perfect relationship and fellowship with God the Father! God came down in the form of Jesus because of His great love for you, and because of His great love for me!

Week 04, Day 04

God the Holy Spirit

In my opinion, God the Holy Spirit is the most overlooked, most misunderstood, and most under-worshipped Person in the Godhead (Holy Trinity).

When we read the Bible, it is pretty evident that the Holy Spirit is very active not only in the lives of believers, but also in the life of the Church. But sometimes, people tend to think that this is something that only applied to the world "back then."

The Holy Spirit is active and alive in the world today as well!

One of the qualities of God is that He does not change—He is the same today as He was yesterday, as He will be tomorrow. If the Holy Spirit of God was different today than He was 2,000 years ago, then that would be a pretty big change.

> Every good and perfect gift is from above, coming down from the Father of the heavenly lights, who does not change like shifting shadows.

James 1:17

While God the Father protects, and God the Son provides payment for our sins and a connection to God the Father, God the Holy Spirit is the presence of God that lives among those who follow Jesus.

> But when the Father sends the Advocate as my representative—that is, the Holy Spirit—he will teach you everything and will remind you of everything I have told you.

John 14:26

He helps us when we are weak. He gives us words when we don't know what to say. He advocates for us. Even when we don't know how to pray, the Holy Spirit steps in and helps us communicate with God the Father through God the Son.

> And the Holy Spirit helps us in our weakness. For example, we don't know what God wants us to pray for. But the Holy Spirit prays for us with groanings that cannot be expressed in words. And the Father who

knows all hearts knows what the Spirit is saying, for the Spirit pleads for us believers in harmony with God's own will.

Romans 8:26-27

The very moment that somebody chooses to start following Jesus, the Holy Spirit allows them to be born into the spiritual family of God.

> Jesus replied, "I assure you, no one can enter the Kingdom of God without being born of water and the Spirit. Humans can reproduce only human life, but the Holy Spirit gives birth to spiritual life. So don't be surprised when I say, 'You must be born again.' The wind blows wherever it wants. Just as you can hear the wind but can't tell where it comes from or where it is going, so you can't explain how people are born of the Spirit."

John 3:5-8

The Spirit, upon moving into the life of a true follower of Jesus, brings with Him gifts, as well as what are known as the "fruits of the Spirit."

> But the Holy Spirit produces this kind of fruit in our lives: love, joy, peace, patience, kindness, goodness,

faithfulness, gentleness, and self-control. There is no law against these things!
Galatians 5:22-23

There is so much more to say about the Holy Spirit, how He works in our lives, and the gifts that He brings. But that is something that we will cover in Week 10 of this book, and in the next book, called *Authentic Community*.

But the important thing to remember for now is that the Holy Spirit is just as much a part of God as God the Father, and as God the Son—Jesus.

The Holy Spirit was extremely active among the early Church in the Book of Acts, and He is the same today as He was 2,000 years ago. And although this may be something that is hard for us to fully grasp, the Holy Spirit promises us that if we will commit to trying to understand and learn more…He will help us!

The Holy Spirit is alive and well. He is here to work in our lives, continually bring us closer to God, and encourage us to live more like Jesus.

Week 04, Day 05

God the Trinity

Over the past four days, we've been covering the individual manifestations of God that make up the Holy Trinity, but today, we are going to talk about the Holy Trinity as a whole. And one of the most difficult things to do when talking about the Holy Trinity is finding a way to adequately describe it…or even understand it.

The Holy Trinity is one of those things that we may never completely understand until we get to heaven.

Obviously, as we've seen, the Bible teaches that God the Father is God, and that Jesus is God, and that the Holy Spirit is God. And while all of those things are true, the Bible also teaches that there is only one true God. And while we may be able to fully understand the individual roles of the members of the Holy

Trinity, trying to fully understand how each member relates to each other while still only being "One God" will drive you crazy. It might be impossible for us to fully grasp.

The Holy Trinity is One God. But the Holy Trinity is also three persons, or "Godheads." It's important for us to understand that this is not three separate Gods. And it's also important for us to realize that the word "Trinity" is a word that early Church leaders made up to try to fully understand the three-in-one nature of God. The word "Trinity" is not actually found anywhere in the Bible—but the *idea* of Trinity is all over the place in the Bible.

The earliest example of where we can find the Trinity is in the very first chapter of the Bible:

> In the beginning God created the heavens and the earth. Then God said, "Let us make human beings in our image, to be like us. They will reign over the fish in the sea, the birds in the sky, the livestock, all the wild animals on the earth, and the small animals that scurry along the ground."
> **Genesis 1:1, 26**

In the above verses, God (Who is one) is talking as if there is more than one talking (let *us* make human beings).

Another passage that not only mentions the three different Godheads, but actually has them interacting, is found in the Gospel of Matthew:

> After his baptism, as Jesus came up out of the water, the heavens were opened and he saw the Spirit of God descending like a dove and settling on him. And a voice from heaven said, "This is my dearly loved Son, who brings me great joy."
> **Matthew 3:16-17**

There have been many attempts by humans to try and explain the Holy Trinity using familiar images...such as how water is water, and there is only one thing truly like water, but that it can manifest itself through liquid, steam, or ice...and while some illustrations like this get some points across, they still fall short. Because water cannot exist in three forms at the same time, while interacting with the other forms.

So, we find ourselves back at the drawing board of faith. And in the long run, we have to be ok with coming to the conclusion that there are certain aspects of God that are not quite comprehendible by our finite (limited) human minds. Because if we fully understood everything there is to know about God... would He still be worth believing in?

Of all the explanations of the Holy Trinity that I've ever heard, I think the one that most adequately and accurately describes the Holy Trinity is this:

The Father is not the Son or the Holy Spirit, but He is God.

The Son is not the Holy Spirit or the Father, but He is God.

The Holy Spirit is not the Father or the Son, but He is God.

All three manifestations of God are all at once separate, but at the same time, all at once God.

And there is only One True God. Make sense?

At the end of the day, this verse brings me comfort:

> Oh, how great are God's riches and wisdom and knowledge! How impossible it is for us to understand his decisions and his ways!
> **Romans 11:33**

To God, three-in-one, be the glory!

Week 04, Day 06

The Kingdom of God

If you've spent any time around any churches or Christian faith communities, or read the Bible, or if you've ever read this book (I know you've done at least one of these things!), then you may have come across the term "Kingdom of God." Maybe you've heard it referred to as the "Kingdom of Heaven."

So…what does that mean? And what is it exactly?

When we're talking big picture, the "Kingdom of God" is basically everything that exists that is under the rule and reign of God.

Do you remember that scene in Disney's *The Lion King* (1994), where Mufasa was showing Simba his kingdom? He said, "Everything the light touches is our kingdom." Simba asked,

"What about that shadowy place?" And Mufasa responded, "That's beyond our borders."

Well…in the Kingdom of God, everything is under the rule and reign of God—even the "shadowy places." There are some places where God is not welcomed…but He is still ruler. There are some hearts that do not belong to Him…but He is still ruler of all.

> The Lord has made the heavens his throne;
>> from there he rules over everything.
>
> **Psalm 103:19**

Even when we're talking about other "kingdoms," such as the rulers of nations and territories, God is ultimately the ruler over all.

> Everyone must submit to governing authorities. For all authority comes from God, and those in positions of authority have been placed there by God.
>
> **Romans 13:1**

That is the Kingdom of God in a general sense—"everything." But we can also talk about what that means in a more specific sense.

In a more specific sense, the Kingdom of God are those people and those places that are living and operating under the submission of God as ruler. Even though there are still many other people and places that still fall under the umbrella of "universe," they do not and will not submit to the authority of God.

Imagine with me that there is a ruler of a country, and this ruler has a big following…but then one day, this ruler ceases to be in charge, and somebody else takes over the leadership of that country. But everybody who really likes the old ruler refuses to accept the new ruler as legitimate. So they say things like, "You're not my ruler! We will never follow you!"

Well…in reality, this new ruler is in charge of all the people and places in that country, whether or not this ruler is seen as legitimate. There are some who will gladly follow, and others who will remain belligerent. But regardless, they are all still citizens of the country, and living under the rule of the governing authority.

So generally speaking, the Kingdom of God is everything in existence. More narrowly speaking, it is those who submit to the Lordship of Jesus, and try to follow His ways. So, in a sense, the Kingdom of God is "Everything the light touches."

Another distinction between the general Kingdom of God vs. the more specific/narrow Kingdom of God is that the universe and everything in it encapsulates both physical and spiritual.

> Look, the highest heavens and the earth and everything in it all belong to the Lord your God.
> **Deuteronomy 10:14**

In a more specific sense, the Kingdom of God is not physical, but Spiritual. It is the hearts and souls of women and men who are living for the glory of Jesus.

> Jesus answered, "My Kingdom is not an earthly kingdom. If it were, my followers would fight to keep me from being handed over to the Jewish leaders. But my Kingdom is not of this world."
> **John 18:36**

Jesus was pretty clear in His teachings that in order to be considered for membership in the Kingdom of God, individuals must be "born again." And being born again simply means being born of the Spirit (as in receiving the Holy Spirit after choosing to follow Jesus). When we are born, physically, that is what the Bible refers to as being born of water. Being "born again" is referred to as being born of the Spirit.

> Jesus replied, "I assure you, no one can enter the Kingdom of God without being born of water and the Spirit. Humans can reproduce only human life, but the

Holy Spirit gives birth to spiritual life. So don't be surprised when I say, 'You must be born again.'"
John 3:5-7

The Kingdom of God is a topic that can sometimes be difficult to grasp and fully understand. I'm certainly still learning and growing in this area. But I hope that today's reading has assisted you in your understanding, and if nothing else, given you some good things to think about.

And I am certain that God, who began the good work within you, will continue his work until it is finally finished on the day when Christ Jesus returns.
Philippians 1:6

As we wrap up today's reading, here's something to consider: Who in your life would you be able to talk to about what you're learning about the Kingdom of God? Is there somebody in your life who might even be interested in joining the Kingdom of God by choosing to follow Jesus?

Many times, it just starts with someone like you sharing with them.

Week 04, Day 07

Bringing Heaven to Earth

Several days ago while we were in the section about talking to God (Week 03, Day 03), I included some verses from something called "The Lord's Prayer," or "The Model Prayer." This is a prayer that Jesus modeled for His followers as a demonstration about how they should pray.

One thing that I'd like to focus on today was included in this model prayer that Jesus gave to us:

> Pray like this:
> Our Father in heaven,
>   may your name be kept holy.
> May your Kingdom come soon.
> May your will be done on earth,
>   as it is in heaven.
> **Matthew 6:9-10**

In yesterday's reading, we focused on what the Kingdom of God is. And so when Jesus prays, "May your Kingdom come soon," He is modeling for us that we should be actively praying for those who are living "in the shadowy place" to move into being part of "everything the light touches."

But after Jesus models praying for the growth of the Kingdom of God, He prays something very interesting (at least, I find it very interesting):

"May your will be done on earth, as it is in heaven."

One of the reasons I find this so interesting is because, for years, I've had a hard time truly understanding what it means. What would it look like if God's people took this prayer seriously? If we actually began doing all we could do to make God's will be done here on earth, as His will is being done in heaven?

When things boil down, I think the best way to think about what "God's will on earth as in heaven" looks like is to more fully understand what heaven looks like.

So, let's explore a little bit about what the Bible says about heaven. Here is a biblical description of heaven, and what it will be like:

I heard a loud shout from the throne, saying, "Look, God's home is now among his people! He will live with them, and they will be his people. God himself will be with them. He will wipe every tear from their eyes, and there will be no more death or sorrow or crying or pain. All these things are gone forever."

Revelation 21:3-4

Stop for one second, close your eyes, and imagine with me a place where tears are wiped away from the eyes of those who are weeping. Imagine a place, the same place, where sorrow is forgotten because of the great joys that are surrounding you. Imagine a place, still the same place, where there are no crying sad tears, because the love and joy and peace that is around you only make you cry happy tears! Imagine a place where hunger pangs no longer exist because people are well fed, and therefore people no longer have to deal with the physical pain of hunger.

Imagine a place where people no longer have to deal with the emotional pain of rejection, because every human is treated with the dignity and respect of being an Image Bearer of God (more on that tomorrow).

Now open your eyes (I'm assuming they were open the whole time because you're still reading this). When you were imagining that place in your head, was it a place that you recognized?

As in…a physical place you've been before but just operating in a different way that it used to operate? Or was that place more of a "heavenly" type place where maybe people were bouncing around on clouds and stuff?

I want to point out two things to you about the place that we just imagined together:

First, this is a description of a potentially real place here on earth. As in, this stuff is attainable, maybe even in your community! This is all stuff that, although it would take great intentionality and quite a bit of elbow grease, could actually come to fruition, if we really, really try!

Second, this place that we just imagined together is actually very similar to the description of heaven we just read about together in **Revelation 21:3-4** (the only thing we are missing is the absence of death, which is not something we can totally prevent this side of heaven).

So…I asked this question near the beginning of today's reading, and I want to ask it again: What would it look like if God's people took this prayer seriously? If we actually began doing all we could do to make God's will be done here on earth, as His will is being done in heaven?

If we are serious about praying this prayer, is there something else we should be doing beyond simply praying it? Is there something you or I could actually physically do to help make this prayer come to fruition?

Or do you think that Jesus' intention was for us to pray for these things to happen, but not actually work towards these things happening?

To me, the answer is obvious. This is something that, in addition to praying about, I should be working towards.

When I identify people in my community who are hungry or hurting, I should pray for them…and then find ways to help them, and find ways to treat them as fellow bearers of the Image of God (more on that tomorrow).

Who is somebody in your life you can talk this through with in the next few days? Are you reading this book with somebody? If so…this would be a good one to talk with about this!

Father God…may your will be done here on earth, specifically in my community, as your will is being done in heaven.

Week 05

The Image of God

Welcome to Week 05 of *Changed By Love*! I hope that this journey has been enjoyable so far, but that it is also stretching you and growing you to be more like Jesus, and to understand more about what it means to follow Jesus! Today's topic is one that I have been passionate about for quite some time, and I'm so excited to explore it with you today! It is the idea that women and men have been created in the "Image of God." And this idea is something that stems all the way back to the very beginning, during creation:

> Then God said, "Let us make human beings in our image, to be like us. They will reign over the fish in the sea, the birds in the sky, the livestock, all the wild animals on the earth, and the small animals that scurry along the ground."

So God created human beings in his own image.
In the image of God he created them;
male and female he created them.

Then God blessed them and said, "Be fruitful and
multiply. Fill the earth and govern it. Reign over the fish
in the sea, the birds in the sky, and all the animals that
scurry along the ground."
Genesis 1:26-28

During the creation account found in Genesis 1, the "crowning
achievement" of God's creation was humankind! And of all the
things that God created, women and men are the only aspect of
creation that got designated as being in the Image of God!

That's not something to take lightly! If you are reading this
sentence (and you're not a robot or a gorilla that learned how to
read), then YOU are created in the Image of God!

Being created in the Image of God means that you and I are
meant to be representative of God here on earth. Now, there's
plenty of debate on what exactly that means, and how far our
likeness with God goes, but...we're not here to argue! So, let's
just have an informative discussion today (and tomorrow) about
what that really means for us, and what we should do about it!

First of all, being made in the Image of God does not necessarily mean that we share a physical resemblance with God (although I know plenty of people who think that about themselves). Instead of being physically created in God's image, it is more mentally, spiritually, emotionally, and even relationally.

Humans are created mentally in the image of God because humans have the ability to grasp more complex ideas such as the future and moral consciousness. We have the ability to persuade others and use reason in our arguments. We have the ability to learn and communicate in multiple languages. We have the ability to be creative and invent things.

Humans are created spiritually in the image of God because humans have the ability to grasp and discuss much deeper things, such as the meaning of life, and existentialism, and sin, and our need for a Savior.

Humans are created emotionally in the image of God because humans have the ability to feel a much wider range of complex emotions than animals typically can. We (some of us) have the ability to even understand the emotions of others, and we know how to appropriately respond.

Humans are created relationally in the image of God because humans have the ability to not only relate to and connect to one another in complex ways, and the ability to relate to and connect to the God of the universe! Since the moment that God created woman and man, we've seen evidence in Scripture that God has not only given us the ability to relationally connect with Him, but that He has desired to be relationally connected with us.

We were created in the Image of God not only to enjoy a relationship with God, but for us to be able to help other Image Bearers of God (fellow humans) to have a relationship with Him as well! I believe that part of bringing Heaven to Earth (see yesterday's reading) is not only fighting for equal treatment for our friends, family, neighbors, but also fighting for them to have a right relationship with God as well!

As we come across fellow humans, who are all also created in the Image of God, we should treat them with the utmost respect and honor. We should help them understand that they are loved, they are valued, and that the God of the universe desires a relationship with them.

Part of how we can do that is with our words. One way that you and I are uniquely created in the Image of God is that our words have great power. Much like we see how God's words have great power in the creation story, your words have great power.

My words have great power.

Take, for example, books. Books are only possible because of the power of words (and sometimes, pictures).

(Sorry that this book does not have pictures).

But our words also have great power because with our words, we can build people and ideas up, or tear people and ideas down.

> No one can tame the tongue. It is restless and evil, full of deadly poison. Sometimes it praises our Lord and Father, and sometimes it curses those who have been made in the image of God.
> **James 3:8-9**

Our words have great power, and they can be used for good or for evil.

Tomorrow, we will talk more about this topic, but today…I challenge you to start making a list of other ways in which we are created in the Image of God!

Share that list with somebody!

Week 05, Day 02

Imago Dei

The first time I ever heard the term "Imago Dei," I was unsure if we were still talking about church stuff, or if the conversation had shifted to Aladdin's talking parrot! But I assure you…we're still talking about church stuff.

"Imago Dei" is simply Latin for "Image of God." This Latin phrase has been used for centuries by church leaders across the globe to refer to the things we discussed in yesterday's reading—how women and men were created in the Image of God.

On the last day of creation, when God created His crowning achievement—humankind—it was also a very personal account of creation. Instead of simply speaking humankind into existence like He did with the rest of creation, He literally breathed humankind into existence.

Then the Lord God formed the man from the dust of the ground. He breathed the breath of life into the man's nostrils, and the man became a living person.

Genesis 2:7

This is yet another way that women and men are different than all the rest of creation. When God breathed life into the material body He had created for humankind, He breathed a soul/spirit into the physical body.

No other part of creation was made with such a personal touch. No other part of creation was made with a soul. Especially cats.

Because we were created with souls, that means that humans were also created morally in the image of God. As humans, we have the ability to fight for justice for our fellow humankind. We also have the ability to have faith in something bigger than ourselves. We are able to engage in something that has become somewhat of a "dirty word" in some circles—religion.

If you claim to be religious but don't control your tongue, you are fooling yourself, and your religion is worthless. Pure and genuine religion in the sight of God the Father means caring for orphans and widows in their distress and refusing to let the world corrupt you.

James 1:26-27

I will be the first to admit that I typically don't have anything good to say about "religion." You may have even heard some people say, "It's not about religion, it's about a relationship with Jesus!"

To that, I say amen!

But…I also need to check myself sometimes because in this Bible verse we just read from the Book of James, it gives us a picture of a religion that is worth engaging in.

And yes, James uses the word "religion."

And as those who were created in the Image of God, we need to use our uniqueness in creation—our moral compass—to help be sure that other humans are created kindly and fairly. We should be on the forefront of fighting for our fellow Image Bearers to be treated with the honor and respect that an Image Bearer of God deserves.

But part of us being created in the Image of God that can be used for evil is…we also have the ability to make choices. Just as God chose to show you and me great grace, we have the ability to makes choices for good…and we have the ability to make choices for bad.

> But God showed his great love for us by sending Christ
> to die for us while we were still sinners.
>
> **Romans 5:8**

Our freedom of choice is evidenced by the fact that humankind
chose sin over a perfect relationship with God.

> When Adam sinned, sin entered the world. Adam's sin
> brought death, so death spread to everyone, for everyone
> sinned.
>
> **Romans 5:12**

Our freedom of choice is also evidenced by the fact that people
like Hitler exist.

And so with the great knowledge that humankind was made in
the Image of God comes great power...and that great power
comes with great choice: How will you choose to use your
uniqueness in creation to affect fellow Image of God Bearers?

How will you use your uniqueness in creation to impact the rest
of humanity, both present generations and future generations?

What can you do to reflect God's Image?

Week 05, Day 03

Reflecting God's Image

Just like the moon reflects the sun, we should reflect the Son.

Ok…stop. I need a graphic designer. Let's print that up and sell it at Hobby Lobby and get rich together!

But in all seriousness…as Christians, you and I are called to reflect the goodness of God. It's part of how we are tasked with bringing Heaven to Earth (see Week 04, Day 07).

> But whenever someone turns to the Lord, the veil is taken away. So all of us who have had that veil removed can see and reflect the glory of the Lord. And the Lord —who is the Spirit—makes us more and more like him as we are changed into his glorious image.
> **2 Corinthians 3:16, 18**

When we become Christians by choosing to start following Jesus, we have the privilege of seeing parts of the goodness of God. And just like this verse says, we should not just receive that goodness…but we should reflect that goodness.

Jesus speaks to this in the most famous sermon He ever gave, called, "The Sermon on the Mount":

> You are the salt of the earth. But what good is salt if it has lost its flavor? Can you make it salty again? It will be thrown out and trampled underfoot as worthless. You are the light of the world—like a city on a hilltop that cannot be hidden. No one lights a lamp and then puts it under a basket. Instead, a lamp is placed on a stand, where it gives light to everyone in the house. In the same way, let your good deeds shine out for all to see, so that everyone will praise your heavenly Father.
> **Matthew 5:13-16**

Have you ever seen someone who, without ever tasting their food, proceeds to dump a whole mountain of salt on it? Or maybe you're the kind of person who, at a Mexican restaurant, dumps pounds of salt on the community chip bowl without asking anybody else if they're ok with it.

Have you ever seen somebody sit down at a table in a restaurant and discover that there is no salt at their table? I have. And I've seen people get downright indignant over it.

Bottom line…people love salt (assuming there is no food sensitivity at play).

And I would be quick to say that I'm not really a salt kind of person…but cook me a meal with no salt in it, and I'll probably be reaching for the shaker!

As Christians, we are called to be the salt of the earth. We are called to bring seasoning that people long for. And the only reason we have any seasoning worth offering is because we are connected to the Head Chef…and oh, He's a good, good Chef!

Not only are we called to be the salt of the earth as a reflection of God, but we are called to be like a city on a hill.

Now, this metaphor might not have the same impact on us as 21st Century American readers…but to the original audience that heard Jesus say these words some 2,000 years ago, a "city on a hill" offered real hope. It offered security. It represented a promise of shelter, a warm bed, and a nice meal (with salt)!

Imagine with me that you are a traveler in the ancient Middle East, and you don't have a horse (because weren't horses invented in America?). You're carrying a lot of stuff with you, on foot, and it's late. You're tired. And it's getting dark outside...

And then in the distance, you see a city on a hill! And you can see it because the lights are on! All of the sudden, you would be filled with hope and a renewed determination to get to where that warm meal was waiting for you.

In a similar way, Christians are called to reflect the hope and hospitality and promises for safety and security to the weary world around us. We are to shine our lights in this way, not because we are good in and of ourselves, but because God is good! And because we are a reflection of His goodness to the world around us!

We were created in the Image of God so that we could reflect God's goodness to those around us.

"In the same way, let your good deeds shine out for all to see, so that everyone will praise your heavenly Father."

Shine bright!

Week 05, Day 04

Head

If you're reading this book, and you're connected to River City Church in Vancouver, WA (the faith family that I currently have the privilege of leading), then you are probably familiar with our definition of discipleship: Becoming more like Jesus with your head, heart, hands, and habits.

We'll talk more about discipleship later, and why it's actually a really exciting thing (it's not boring or scary like I always assumed growing up), but over the next few days, we're going to focus on what it looks like to become more like Jesus with our head, heart, hands, and habits.

And we'll start with "head."

I've seen many examples of Christians and churches that believe the only way to become more like Jesus is by learning more stuff.

Reading more books. Memorizing more verses. Knowing all the definitions to all the big words like "transubstantiation."

And yes…all of those things are important, but I don't think we can stop there. But instead of making a case *against* filling your head with knowledge, let me make a case *for* it.

There are several Bible verses that talk about the usefulness of knowing Scripture, and being intimately aware of what it says. One such verse that comes to mind is:

> Study this Book of Instruction continually. Meditate on it day and night so you will be sure to obey everything written in it. Only then will you prosper and succeed in all you do.
> **Joshua 1:8**

In this verse, we are instructed to meditate on God's Word day and night. That sounds like a pretty intense study session to me! Also listen to what the early Church leader, Paul, wrote to his protégé Timothy:

> You have been taught the holy Scriptures from childhood, and they have given you the wisdom to receive the salvation that comes by trusting in Christ Jesus. All

Scripture is inspired by God and is useful to teach us what is true and to make us realize what is wrong in our lives. It corrects us when we are wrong and teaches us to do what is right. God uses it to prepare and equip his people to do every good work.
2 Timothy 3:15-17

Through the study of Scripture comes the knowledge of Jesus that leads us to salvation! That's pretty important! But not only does it lead to salvation, but it can lead to right living, and it can help us equip those around us to do good works.

All that is made possible because of the study of Scripture. It is so vitally important! And not just studying it...but memorizing it!

I have hidden your word in my heart,
that I might not sin against you.
Psalm 119:11

When temptation comes our way, certain Bible verses that we may have committed to memory (or recently studied) will pop up in our heads and help us to stay on the straight and narrow! But...as important as studying Scripture is, we need to be careful about not allowing the Scripture to simply go to our heads...and stay in our heads.

> But don't just listen to God's word. You must do what it says. Otherwise, you are only fooling yourselves.
> **James 1:22**

The Bible is clear. If we are successful in listening to, or studying Scripture, but we fail to do what it says...we have missed the mark. In other words, early Church leader James says we are simply fooling ourselves.

Fooling ourselves how?

I think it's safe to say that sometimes, with great knowledge, comes a pretty high view of self. If I read the manual from front to back, I am tempted to believe that I have the best working knowledge of whatever gadget I'm studying, even if I have never actually worked with whatever gadget I was reading about.

> ...while knowledge makes us feel important, it is love that strengthens the church. Anyone who claims to know all the answers doesn't really know very much. But the person who loves God is the one whom God recognizes.
> **1 Corinthians 8:1b-3**

If we study the Bible until we are blue in the face, but fail to actually live any of it out, then we have missed the mark.

Imagine with me for one moment that I am your father (insert asthmatic breathing sounds). And, as your parent, I am asking you to go clean your room. And maybe this is something that I have even been asking you to do for several days, or weeks…or even months. "Go clean your room!"

Now imagine with me that you go to the library and check out some books about how to best clean your room. And you read those books. And then, you do an internet search. Not only do you search "how to clean your room," but you search "BEST way to clean your room."

You compile a bunch of articles, even print a few out, and make some good highlights and notes. And after all your study, you even decide to make a nice presentation, complete with a slideshow.

After everything is said and done, you will have really done a great job of filling your head with knowledge about how to clean your room. But at the end of the day, even if you know the most about best practices for tidying up…would anybody in their right mind consider any of that a success?

The clear answer is no. And so we must not fall into the same trap when it comes to living out our Christian faith.

Week 05, Day 05

Heart

When we discuss "becoming more like Jesus with our hearts," I think it's safe to assume that you don't think that I am talking about the vital, blood-pumping organ that sits inside your chest. Instead, I am talking about your passions, and your love for people (non-romantically).

As we saw in yesterday's reading…if our study of Scripture doesn't make it past our heads, then we have missed the mark. Even if you have spent more hours than anybody else studying Theology (the study of God), and memorizing terms, and winning debates, and showing off your knowledge…it is all for naught.

When we are discussing the importance of allowing Scripture to not just fill your head, but to actually change the way that you love, I cannot think of a better passage to share with you than than this one:

If I could speak all the languages of earth and of angels, but didn't love others, I would only be a noisy gong or a clanging cymbal. If I had the gift of prophecy, and if I understood all of God's secret plans and possessed all knowledge, and if I had such faith that I could move mountains, but didn't love others, I would be nothing.

1 Corinthians 13:1-2

If I have all the knowledge but no love...I am nothing.

I don't know about you, but there have been many times when I've demonstrated my head knowledge on some particular issue...and while I may come across as the most informed person in the room, I also come across as the biggest jerk in the room. The more we study, and the more knowledge we acquire, the more we need to be intentional about making sure that we apply that knowledge with a healthy dose of heart.

But before we simply just add "heart" into the equation, we must make sure that the heart we are talking about is a heart that has been transformed by Jesus. Because hearts aren't in-and-of themselves always good things.

> The human heart is the most deceitful of all things,
> and desperately wicked. Who really knows how bad it is?
> **Jeremiah 17:9**

We have to remember that our hearts are naturally inclined to sin. And if we let our hearts go unchecked and untransformed by the love of Jesus, then our hearts will use our knowledge to put forward ideas that are not at all defined by love or the way of Jesus.

But...after we are truly transformed by Jesus, He gives us this beautiful promise:

> And I will give you a new heart, and I will put a new spirit in you. I will take out your stony, stubborn heart and give you a tender, responsive heart. And I will put my Spirit in you so that you will follow my decrees and be careful to obey my regulations.
> **Ezekiel 36:26-27**

A heart that is transformed by Jesus is the kind of heart that we're after. And what's one of the best ways to have a heart that is transformed by Jesus? Simple..by spending time with Jesus!

One way to spend time with Jesus is by reading and studying His Word! But another way is through prayer and meditation.

We talked about prayer a lot in Week 03, and I would encourage you to revisit your highlights from that section. Christian meditation is the process of not just studying and/or memorizing

Scripture, but really spending quality time thinking on it, praying about it, and trying to find ways to say the same thing, but in your own words.

Christian meditation is about filling your mind with the Words of God (vs. Eastern meditation, which is all about emptying your mind).

So, you finish your presentation of how to clean your room, and you see the clear disappointment on my face because your room is still not clean. So you decide to go and have a discussion with a close family friend...let's call him Yoda.

Yoda takes you to a swamp that kind of resembles your room that you need to clean, and he demonstrates to you why having a clean room is important. You are able to see the clear benefits to having a clean room, and...now that you think about it, you really actually prefer a clean room!

You would maybe even say that you're in love with the idea of having a clean room! So, you excitedly come back home and proudly announce that you really love living in a clean room now! And not only do you understand the benefits of having a clean room...cleaning is something that you would really actually enjoy doing!

If it stopped there…would anybody in their right mind consider any of that a success? I mean, sure…we're moving in the right direction, but we are not there yet.

The clear answer is no. And so we must not fall into the same trap when it comes to living out our Christian faith. Love is so, so, so very important! But…we cannot stop with love.

We must become more like Jesus with our head, and we need to keep continually doing so…but we cannot stop there.

We must become more like Jesus with our heart, and we need to keep continually doing so…but we cannot stop there.

Tomorrow, we will talk about one of the ingredients that is still missing. But while we're waiting for tomorrow, what are some things you can do to help ensure that your heart doesn't start slipping back into its natural, desperately wicked state?

Week 05, Day 06

Hands

You've done more studying on the topic of clean rooms than anybody you know, and you're to the point in your life where you actually prefer a clean room. You would even say you *love* a clean room. But…is your room clean?

> But don't just listen to God's word. You must do what it says. Otherwise, you are only fooling yourselves. For if you listen to the word and don't obey, it is like glancing at your face in a mirror. You see yourself, walk away, and forget what you look like. But if you look carefully into the perfect law that sets you free, and if you do what it says and don't forget what you heard, then God will bless you for doing it.
> **James 1:22-25**

Sometimes, it is so easy to fall into the trap of not actually putting action behind our words. It's not that we're bad people (that was a poor theological statement…we *are* bad people), but…sometimes we mean the best, yet don't ever end up following through with what we intended to do.

And then we comfort ourselves by quoting that verse that we memorized years ago, "It's the thought that counts!"

But wait…that's not a Bible verse, but it is what you told that friend when they gave you a gift that you really did not want or need! Because when it comes to "It's the thought that counts," let me share with you what the Bible says about that:

> What good is it, dear brothers and sisters, if you say you have faith but don't show it by your actions? Can that kind of faith save anyone? Suppose you see a brother or sister who has no food or clothing, and you say, "Goodbye and have a good day; stay warm and eat well"—but then you don't give that person any food or clothing. What good does that do?
>
> Just as the body is dead without breath, so also faith is dead without good works.
> **James 2:14-16, 26**

If it's the thought that counts, then there would be no hungry or hurting people in our communities. But…it's not the thought that counts. If it was the thought that counts, then your room would have been cleaned a long time ago. But…I think you get it.

Sometimes, I hear people argue about how this point is not really all that important, and that it's maybe important for some people, but not every Christian really needs to get active with their hands.

It's as if some Christians think that they can be the designated thinkers, while everybody else does the work.

One justification that I've heard about this is: "It's pretty much just James who says all the stuff about 'faith without works is dead.' That idea really isn't found elsewhere in the Bible."

Well, please allow me to not only share with you where else this idea is found in the Bible…but to also share that these Words came straight from the mouth of Jesus!

> Then the King will say to those on his right, 'Come, you who are blessed by my Father, inherit the Kingdom prepared for you from the creation of the world. For I was hungry, and you fed me. I was thirsty, and you gave me a drink. I was a stranger, and you invited me into your

home. I was naked, and you gave me clothing. I was sick, and you cared for me. I was in prison, and you visited me.'

Then these righteous ones will reply, 'Lord, when did we ever see you hungry and feed you? Or thirsty and give you something to drink? Or a stranger and show you hospitality? Or naked and give you clothing? When did we ever see you sick or in prison and visit you?'

And the King will say, 'I tell you the truth, when you did it to one of the least of these my brothers and sisters, you were doing it to me!'
Matthew 25:34-40

It doesn't matter how much I think about it, or how smart I am. It doesn't matter how much I love it, or how passionate I am. At the end of the day, if my room doesn't get cleaned, then I have failed at my assigned task.

We cannot stop with thoughts and prayers. We cannot stop with love and compassion.

As obedient Christ followers, we must be people of action. Let's clean our room!

Week 05, Day 07

Habits

Ok, so your room is finally clean! Awesome! But…what about next week?

Without the right habits in place, we will have to go through the same song and dance in just a few days, and we'll be right back where we started. You can give a man a fish…

When we are following Jesus, and becoming more like Him with our head, heart, and hands, we're definitely on the right path! But now, we need to start following Him with our habits as well! Sometimes, you'll hear these referred to as "spiritual disciplines." But don't let that term scare you. Spiritual Disciplines are primarily about repeated behaviors that help you to become more like Jesus with your habits. Anybody can do them, they just take some dedicated time, and a real commitment.

Speaking of teaching a man to fish...when Jesus interrupted the lives of those that He would call to follow Him, He didn't simply ask them to commit to doing a nice deed or putting on a nice event. He didn't ask them to learn the entire Bible by memory, or even to love people better (although that would come later).

When Jesus called people to follow Him, He asked them to change their entire way of life.

> Jesus called out to them, "Come, follow me, and I will show you how to fish for people!" And they left their nets at once and followed him.
> **Matthew 4:19-20**

The promise that Jesus gave them was not that He would teach them a better way of playing the game...but that He would change the game entirely! Jesus asked them to throw down their old habits (they left their nets...this was a lifestyle they were leaving behind), and they followed Him.

But Jesus didn't just ask for life change from His most committed followers. He even asked for life change from people He'd never see again. There is a story of a woman who was caught in a lifestyle of sin and, even though some scholars believe she became a disciple of Jesus, others disagree. It's not something that we know for sure. But…what we do know for sure is that after Jesus came into contact with this woman, He asked her to change her habits. He asked her to change the way she lived.

> Go and sin no more.
> **John 8:11b**

Jesus had a habit of changing people's habits.
(Stop. Print. Hobby Lobby!)

One time while Jesus was talking about one of the most grievous of sins—murder—He asked all those who were listening to change their habits:

> You have heard that our ancestors were told, 'You must not murder. If you commit murder, you are subject to judgment.' But I say, if you are even angry with someone, you are subject to judgment!
> **Matthew 5:21-22a**

If we are truly going to be followers of Jesus, then our behaviors cannot be limited to our head, heart, or hands. Our behaviors must extend through to our habits. This is not something that should come as a surprise to us, because it was one of the main directives Jesus gave us when He gave us our final marching

164

orders, "The Great Commission" (more on this tomorrow).

> Jesus came and told his disciples, "I have been given all authority in heaven and on earth. Therefore, go and make disciples of all the nations, baptizing them in the name of the Father and the Son and the Holy Spirit. Teach these new disciples to obey all the commands I have given you. And be sure of this: I am with you always, even to the end of the age."
> **Matthew 28:18-20**

We are not simply commanded to just all that Jesus commanded…that's stopping at your head. Instead, we are to teach new disciples *to obey*.

That means as disciples, we should be obeying.

And it should be habitual.

As a parent, I don't want my kids to just learn about cleaning their rooms, and I don't want them to just like having a clean room. When my kids actually clean their rooms, it's great! But ultimately…I want my kids to have habits that lead to clean living, and for those habits to lead to a perpetually clean room.

Impossible? No.

Improbable? Yes…because our hearts are desperately wicked.

But it doesn't mean that we can't aim for it.

Speaking of head, heart, hands, and habits, I'm going to let you in on a little secret! When you are reading this book, that is focused on building up your head. When you meet up with a friend or mentor to discuss what you are reading, that reflection is focused on building up your heart. When you check off items back in the thresholds section, that is focused on building up your hands!

And when you start going through this book, or the book *Curious?* with somebody else, then that works out your habits muscle!

So, how are you doing with your reading buddy?

How are you doing with the thresholds section?

And are you passing on what you're learning, and helping someone else do the same?

Week 06

The Great Co-Mission(s)

Have you ever been with somebody who knew the end was near? Maybe they were nearing the end of a battle with a terminal illness, or maybe they were just really advanced in years and they knew their time was near…I've often heard stories of people in such situations gathering their loved ones close and saying what may be remembered as their "final words."

Typically, those "final words" are remembered forever by whoever received them. They were very meaningful. They were important. They were the dying wishes of somebody who was loved.

Jesus knew that His time on earth was about to end. He was not about to die (that had already happened, and He came back), but He was about to ascend into heaven where He would be seated at the right hand of the Father. So…His time on earth was almost over. And these were His final words:

Jesus came and told his disciples, "I have been given all authority in heaven and on earth. Therefore, go and make disciples of all the nations, baptizing them in the name of the Father and the Son and the Holy Spirit. Teach these new disciples to obey all the commands I have given you. And be sure of this: I am with you always, even to the end of the age."

Matthew 28:18-20

You may know this passage as "The Great Commission." If you're like me…what does the word "commission" even mean? Well, it's simple, really! It's the prefix "co," as in something that you do together, combined with the word "mission," as in an assignment. Then, add an extra "m" in there because English is confusing, and you get the word "commission!"

But it's really a beautiful word, because the "co" part refers to the fact that Jesus is on mission with us! We literally get to team up with Jesus to carry out the final mission that He gave us with His final words here on earth!

What a privilege and an honor!

We're going to spend some time over the next few days breaking this co-mission down into bite-sized pieces, but just know that it is an assignment we've been given as followers of Jesus, and we are not alone in our efforts!

As Jesus was headed out of here, He said another powerful message. This one is found in the book of Acts, which records the immediate aftermath of when Jesus left, and the very first Church in all of history! Here is the passage:

> So when the apostles were with Jesus, they kept asking him, "Lord, has the time come for you to free Israel and restore our kingdom?" He replied, "The Father alone has the authority to set those dates and times, and they are not for you to know. But you will receive power when the Holy Spirit comes upon you. And you will be my witnesses, telling people about me everywhere—in Jerusalem, throughout Judea, in Samaria, and to the ends of the earth."
>
> **Acts 1:6-8**

After Jesus was raised from the dead, His disciples were pretty pumped up because they thought that they were about to conquer their corner of the world, starting by physically overcoming their Roman oppressors and liberating the nation of Israel. So His followers asked Him (and kept asking Him), "Lord, has the time come for us to make Israel great again?"

Jesus responded simply and gently, "Friends, we are not to establish a physical kingdom. Instead, we are here for spiritual global domination!"

And then Jesus caps it off with this: "Oh, and my Holy Spirit will be with you…but it's up to you to lead the charge!"

No biggie!

Here's the really exciting (and slightly terrifying) part of all of this: both of these co-missions were not only for His eleven disciples (twelve, minus Judas), but both of these co-missions are meant for you and me as well!

These co-missions are meant for all followers of Jesus, across all time, and across all geographic borders!

And while this task might seem daunting…Jesus is with us until the end! If you're a follower of Jesus, then His Holy Spirit is living inside you right now, and He is ready to do this with you!

Are you ready? Let's go!

Week 06, Day 02

Making Disciples

These days, making disciples of Jesus sometimes seems like a really daunting task that only super educated, highly skilled and specially trained professionals are able to do. But the reality is… none of that is true.

Making disciples is something that Jesus wants from each and every one of His followers. He's not just looking for pros (and honestly, sometimes the pros just get in the way of what Jesus is wanting to do), but He is looking for those who are willing to be used by Him.

"But Ryan," you might say, "I don't know enough stuff! I don't even have any Bible college degrees!"

Well, I think you're in good company. Allow me to explain.

The eleven disciples (twelve, minus Judas) that Jesus commanded to make disciples of all nations did not have Bible college degrees, either. In fact, they were just ordinary men, who probably didn't even finish high school.

You see, in modern day America, there are a lot of "professional Christians" who try to tell you that the work of making disciples is only reserved for the theologians and scholars. Well…if that's the case, then Jesus picked the wrong people.

And spoiler alert, Jesus never picks the wrong people. And, another spoiler, you are one of the people that Jesus picked!

When it comes down to it, making disciples is less about information transfer (although that's important) than it is a life-on-life relationship with somebody who may be just a step or two behind where you are.

Discipleship does not have to happen in a classroom setting (Paul did that sometimes, but Jesus never did). Instead, it should happen more naturally. Kind of like "hanging out," but on purpose instead of just because.

One of the most beautiful verses I've ever seen about how to make disciples was written by Paul, the great disciple maker:

And you should imitate me, just as I imitate Christ.
1 Corinthians 11:1

Some translations say "Follow me as I follow Christ."

Now realistically…how hard does that sound? Because if you're anything like me, you might be asking, "But wait…is that it?"

In a nutshell, yes. That's it.

There are a few more things that can be helpful in your discipleship journey, and I'm certain that if you start being faithful in this way that your discipleship process might take more "shape" over the years…but yes. This is a great starting point.

It really can be that simple!

But I'm going to do my best to make it even simpler for you and give you a step-by-step guide to follow.

Step 1: Pray

If you're not sure who God would want you to start discipling, then the very first step is to pray for guidance on who to disciple. Remember…you don't need any special training in order to be able to start making disciples. So don't get nervous. And if you do get nervous (it happens to the best of us), just don't forget Who your copilot is on the co-mission!

After you determine who the Lord may want you to start discipling, begin praying for them by name (privately, not in big prayer groups). Paul was faithful to pray for those whom he had a discipleship relationship with:

> So we keep on praying for you, asking our God to enable you to live a life worthy of his call. May he give you the power to accomplish all the good things your faith prompts you to do. Then the name of our Lord Jesus will be honored because of the way you live, and you will be honored along with him. This is all made possible because of the grace of our God and Lord, Jesus Christ.
> **2 Thessalonians 1:11-12**

Why don't you take some time today and simply pray. Pray that the Lord would illuminate somebody in your life who He would want you to disciple. Pray that He would give you the courage to not be afraid to enter into this relationship.

Pray that He would protect you and them against attacks from the enemy, who does not want to see more disciples made.

Week 06, Day 03

Making Disciples, Part 2

After you've determined who the Lord wants you to start discipling, and after you've spent some time praying for them (it may be a small group of people instead of an individual), then it's time to move to the next step!

Step 2: Ask

Now, believe it or not, there are actually ways to do this without coming across as a weird religious nut job. I've found that questions like "Would you like to imitate me as I imitate Christ and become my disciple?" typically don't do too well. Instead of asking something formal, I suggest approaching the individual that the Lord has placed on your heart and ask something along the lines of: "Would you like to get coffee or lunch together sometime soon? And maybe we can talk about some deeper things I've been thinking through? I'd love to hear your thoughts on some of the things I've been thinking about!"

First of all, people love sharing their ideas on things. Second, people typically like getting coffee or lunch with somebody they may look up to! So chances are, they'll say yes! If they say no, it's not time to abort the mission just yet…simple regather and try again at Step 1.

Remember that not everybody will say yes. Here's an example of when Jesus asked somebody to follow Him. We're not sure for certain, but it can be argued with reasonable certainty that this person did not say yes to following Jesus:

> As they were walking along, someone said to Jesus, "I will follow you wherever you go." But Jesus replied, "Foxes have dens to live in, and birds have nests, but the Son of Man has no place even to lay his head."

> He said to another person, "Come, follow me." The man agreed, but he said, "Lord, first let me return home and bury my father." But Jesus told him, "Let the spiritually dead bury their own dead! Your duty is to go and preach about the Kingdom of God."

Another said, "Yes, Lord, I will follow you, but first let me say good-bye to my family." But Jesus told him, "Anyone who puts a hand to the plow and then looks back is not fit for the Kingdom of God."
Luke 9:57-62

Before we move on, here's a pro tip: Jesus will not be your co-pilot if you're doing this to try and score a date. The Holy Spirit is not there to be your wingman as you try to pick up romantic partners. So...go ahead and store that little nugget away in the back of your noggin in case it'll ever be useful to you.

Step 3: Pray (again)

Don't skip this step.

You can never underestimate the power of talking with your co-pilot while you're flying a mission. Spend some time in prayer before your first meetup. Spend some time meditating on some Scripture as well, and allow the Holy Spirit to speak to you, and to reassure you that He is with you.

Remember, if you try, there is no way to "fail" this mission, as long as Jesus is riding shotgun! If you get nervous, here is some Scripture that can serve as a comfort to you:

Don't worry about anything; instead, pray about everything. Tell God what you need, and thank him for all he has done. Then you will experience God's peace, which exceeds anything we can understand. His peace will guard your hearts and minds as you live in Christ Jesus.
Philippians 4:6-7

Step 4: Meet

If you've made it this far, then trust me…this is the easy part!

Ask them how they are! Ask them what they're celebrating in life these days! Ask them about what's causing them pain, and pray with them. Then, ask if you can read some Scripture together (if they're not yet a believer in Jesus, maybe go through the *Curious?* book together instead)!

Let us think of ways to motivate one another to acts of love and good works. And let us not neglect our meeting together, as some people do, but encourage one another, especially now that the day of his return is drawing near.
Hebrews 10:24-25

Step 5: Reflect

Make sure you don't skip this step! It's important to reflect on what you guys just read together!

Ask some good questions that will help get the juices flowing! If you're not sure what to ask, here is a good place to start:

1. What do you think this passage tells us about God/Jesus and His plan?
2. What do you think this passage tells us about humans?
3. What do you think the passage tells us about you and me?
4. If we really believe this is the Word of God, then what should we do about it?

If the conversation goes a different direction than these questions suggest, as long as it is still on topic, by all means chase those bunny trails! Remember, the relational aspect of what you're doing is far more important than getting though the list of questions.

Step 6: Pray & Set a Next Time

End your time in prayer for each other, and ask the Lord to give you strength to follow through with any commitments made, or any revelations realized. Then, set a time to meet again!

And now, you're making disciples! You and your co-pilot aren't too bad at this after all!

Week 06, Day 04

Being a Disciple

The Apostle Paul was an early Church leader who went down as perhaps the greatest church starter and disciple-maker of all time (Jesus was not included in this poll). One of Paul's primary disciples was a young man named Timothy.

Check out this verse that Paul wrote to Timothy about how to effectively make disciples:

> You have heard me teach things that have been confirmed by many reliable witnesses. Now teach these truths to other trustworthy people who will be able to pass them on to others.
> **2 Timothy 2:2**

This is such an exciting verse on discipleship because it shows the power of multiplication. You may not have even realized this, but there are four distinct generations of disciples that are mentioned in this one verse alone.

Go ahead and read it one more time—see if you can spot all four generations of discipleship!

Did you see them? Here they are:

- Paul (that's the "me" in this verse)
- Timothy (that's the "you" in this verse)
- Trustworthy people
- Others

The power of faithful disciples making faithful disciples really is such a powerful thing! And this is something that you can be involved in as well.

But one thing that I want to be sure you understand is this: If you are going to make disciples, you need to be discipled.

In order to be pouring out to trustworthy people, who will be able to pour out into others, you need somebody to be pouring into you and helping you grow. You need a "Paul" in your life.

You and I both need a Paul in our lives.

One of the goals of discipleship is for us to be able to go deeper with the people that we are discipling. And if we are going to be able to go deeper, then we need to be prepared.

If you don't know how to swim, then floaties are a must. And a "Paul" type figure will help you find the right ones.

> So let us stop going over the basic teachings about Christ again and again. Let us go on instead and become mature in our understanding. Surely we don't need to start again with the fundamental importance of repenting from evil deeds and placing our faith in God.
> **Hebrews 6:1**

Not only will a "Paul" type figure help you go deeper, and help you be prepared to go deeper with those who you are discipling, but she or he will also be there for when tough questions come up. And when tough questions do come up (they will), be sure to be honest. Tell them you don't know. But go to your discipler and see if they can help you find an answer to bring back to your disciple.

One of the things that I've realized is that there are no new questions under the sun.

> History merely repeats itself. It has all been done before. Nothing under the sun is truly new. Sometimes people

say, "Here is something new!" But actually it is old; nothing is ever truly new.

Ecclesiastes 1:9-10

But if questions do come up that really, truly, are new, you'll want help navigating those. Somebody to help walk alongside you while you walk alongside someone else is vital in making sure that you don't accidentally start teaching heresy (teachings that go against what Jesus was really about).

Here is what Paul told one of his other disciples, Titus:

> As for you, Titus, promote the kind of living that reflects wholesome teaching. Teach the older men to exercise self-control, to be worthy of respect, and to live wisely. They must have sound faith and be filled with love and patience.

Titus 2:1-2

"Wholesome teaching" is just a fancy word for "not heresy."

Find somebody who will help walk this journey with you. Trust me, it will be well worth it!

Week 06, Day 05

Learning the Bible

Moving forward, I am hoping that we are on the same page as far as "head knowledge" being very important, but that it is also vitally important for the knowledge to be well balanced with your heart, your hands, and your habits!

Imagine with me that you need to clean your room…

But seriously, learning the Bible is something that is really important (it is, after all, God's Word to you and to me). But let's agree to not let that knowledge just stay in your head.

Take a second to flip back a few weeks to Week 03, Days 04 and 05, and revisit your highlights. Read those two days again if you need to, but all the tools that you need to effectively study the Bible are contained there and in Day 07 of the same week.

Using those tools will help you to more fully understand and apply what you're reading in the Bible, but today's focus is less on how to study individual passages, and more on how to navigate the Bible as a whole.

Now...the Bible is a pretty big book. If you've only got a copy on your phone, you may not yet realize just how big it is. But at first glance, it can be pretty overwhelming.

One of the most helpful things I did when I was first learning the Bible was to break it down into smaller, bite-sized pieces. Learning what different kinds of literature are included, and where to find them.

Also, not to be confusing, but the Bible is less of a book, and more of a collection of books. There are 66 books that together make up the modern day Protestant Christian Bible. How those books were selected to be a part of this collection is a much bigger story for another day, but we trust that the Holy Spirit played His part in bringing them together. We trust that the whole Bible is worth studying.

> All Scripture is inspired by God and is useful to teach us what is true and to make us realize what is wrong in our lives. It corrects us when we are wrong and teaches us to

do what is right. God uses it to prepare and equip his people to do every good work.
1 Timothy 3:16-17

So let's break down the Bible into more manageable sections. The first distinction to make is between the "Old Testament," and the "New Testament." You may hear these sometimes referred to as "Old Covenant," and "New Covenant." The Old Testament (OT) is on the left side of your Bible, and the New Testament (NT) is on the right side of your Bible. The most basic difference between the OT and the NT is that the OT is everything that happened before Jesus became flesh and lived as a human. The NT is after Jesus became flesh.

So the OT is looking forward to a Savior who would "one day come," while the NT is looking back at Jesus, His teachings, and how we should respond both personally, and as faith families that follow Jesus. Go to the table of contents of your Bible, and briefly familiarize yourself with which book titles fall into which section—OT or NT. That will be very helpful in your journey.

Next, let's break it down even further into "genres." I've found it helpful to break things down into eight different genres, keeping in mind that some books are more than one genre.

Historical Narrative

These historical narratives are found in both the OT and the NT, and they are retellings of real, factual, historical events. The books that fall into this category are:

OT: Genesis, Exodus, Numbers, Deuteronomy, Joshua, Judges, Ruth, 1-2 Samuel, 1-2 Kings, 1-2 Chronicles, Ezra, Nehemiah, Esther, parts of Job and parts of the Prophets (more on that later).

NT: Matthew, Mark, Luke, John, and Acts.

Law

The books of Law are found in the OT. They are filled with God's commands to the nation Israel, and others who were considered His "covenant people." The books that fall into this category are:

OT: Leviticus, parts of Exodus, Numbers, and Deuteronomy.

Poetry

The books of Poetry are found in the OT, and they are filled with Scripture written in verse form. Some originally meant to be read as poetry, others originally intended to be songs of praise, songs of lament, songs of thanksgiving, and songs of celebration! The books that fall into this category are:

OT: Psalms, Song of Solomon, Lamentations, and mixed in are some books that fit into the OT Narrative genre.

Wisdom Literature

The books of Wisdom Literature are found in the OT, and they are filled with wise sayings and teachings from wise people who were following God. The books that fall into this category are:

OT: Proverbs, Job, and Ecclesiastes

Prophecy

The books of Prophecy are found in the OT (although you'll come across prophecy in the NT through certain people like John the Baptist and the Apostle John). These books of Prophecy are filled with teachings from God, passed through His messengers, and are about things that are going to happen (or were going to happen, and have since already happened). And this genre is actually broken down into two sub-genres: Major and minor prophets (the difference being the size of the book). The books that fall into this category are:

OT Major Prophets: Isaiah, Jeremiah, Ezekiel, and Daniel.

OT Minor Prophets: Hosea, Joel, Amos, Obadiah, Jonah, Micah, Nahum, Habakkuk, Zephaniah, Haggai, Zechariah, and Malachi.

Apocalyptic Literature

The books of Apocalyptic Literature are found in both the OT and the NT, and they are filled with descriptions of what the "end times" will be like. The books that fall into this category are:

OT: Parts of Isaiah, Jeremiah, Ezekiel, Joel, Zechariah, and Daniel.

NT: Primarily Revelation, but also parts of Matthew (chapters 24-25), Mark (chapter 13), and 2 Thessalonians (chapter 2).

Gospels

The Gospel books are found in the NT, and they are filled with stories and accounts of the life and ministry of Jesus. The books that fall into this category are:

NT: Matthew, Mark, Luke, and John.

The Letters (or Epistles)

The Letters are just that…letters that were written to both specific individuals and specific geographically defined faith families. These letters were later turned into books that were passed around for study. The letters, or Epistles, are found in the NT, and they are filled with both specific and general instruction for how to live out the faith. The books that fall into this category are:

NT: Romans, 1 Corinthians, 2 Corinthians, Galatians, Ephesians, Philippians, Colossians, 1-2 Thessalonians, 1-2 Timothy, Titus, Philemon, Hebrews, James, 1-2 Peter, 1-3 John, and Jude.

I know that's a lot to take in…but don't stress too much over it. Just familiarize yourself with these different genres, what they are, and basically which books fall into which genres.

Knowing these things will help you better navigate your Bible, *especially* if you're ever in a situation where you're trying to navigate it without the internet!

Week 06, Day 06

Learning the Gospel

The word "Gospel" is not one we hear often, but it simply means "good news." When we are talking about books of the Bible (Matthew, Mark, Luke, and John), those are known as "Gospels."

For instance, the "Gospel of Matthew" is the "Good news as told by Matthew."

But when we are talking about *the* Gospel, it is referring to something much greater than a book! The Gospel is the Good News of Jesus for humankind!

So when we talk about learning the Gospel, it's not so much about learning the structure of the books of Matthew, Mark, etc., but it's about learning the Good News of Jesus!

1. Humans (and sin)

The first thing you need to know to really learn the Gospel is that it is, like most good news, a solution to a problem. And the problem that the Gospel addresses is the problem of sin.

We've talked about sin plenty of times so far in this book and in the last book, *Curious?*, but sin is a real problem for humanity.

> As the Scriptures say, "No one is righteous— not even one. For everyone has sinned; we all fall short of God's glorious standard."
> **Romans 3:10, 23**

Because each and every woman and man on earth is a sinner, that creates a world full of sin. And, like most bad things, with sin comes consequences, or a penalty.

> The person who sins is the one who will die. The child will not be punished for the parent's sins, and the parent will not be punished for the child's sins. Righteous people will be rewarded for their own righteous behavior, and wicked people will be punished for their own wickedness.
> **Ezekiel 18:20**

Sin is a real problem that doesn't simply just lead to negative consequences, but it actually leads to death.

Temptation comes from our own desires, which entice us and drag us away. These desires give birth to sinful actions. And when sin is allowed to grow, it gives birth to death.
James 1:14-15

2. God

When we contrast our sinful nature with the nature of God, that is where the real problem comes in. God is holy, and He is separate from sin. The OT Prophet, Habakkuk, had this to say about how holy God is:

> But you are pure and cannot stand the sight of evil.
> **Habakkuk 1:13a**

In fact, when Jesus (God the Son) was hanging on the cross, about to die for our sins, there was a moment when He bore the burden of all our sins. And it was at that moment that, because there was so much sin on Jesus, God the Father had to look away.

> At noon, darkness fell across the whole land until three o'clock. At about three o'clock, Jesus called out with a loud voice, "Eli, Eli, lema sabachthani?" which means "My God, my God, why have you abandoned me?"
> **Matthew 27:45-46**

CHANGED BY LOVE

3. Jesus

Speaking of Jesus hanging on the cross…the reason He did that was because sin demanded a penalty. There is a cost involved. And the price to cover the penalty of sin is blood.

> In fact, according to the law of Moses, nearly everything was purified with blood. For without the shedding of blood, there is no forgiveness.
> **Hebrews 9:22**

That's why in the OT you see people making animal sacrifices for their sins. Those sacrifices were literally to pay for their sins. Because sin demands payment.

> The life of the body is in its blood. I have given you the blood on the altar to purify you, making you right with the Lord. It is the blood, given in exchange for a life, that makes purification possible.
> **Leviticus 17:11**

But an animal sacrifice only went so far to pay for human sins. So because of that, animals had to be sacrificed on a regular basis, because people were sinning on a regular basis.

> But only the high priest ever entered the Most Holy Place, and only once a year. And he always offered blood

for his own sins and for the sins the people had committed in ignorance.

Hebrews 9:7

Since that blood sacrifice wasn't sufficient to cover all of the sins of humankind—past, present, and future—Jesus came in the flesh for the purpose of making the ultimate sacrifice for you and me.

> Christ suffered for our sins once for all time. He never sinned, but he died for sinners to bring you safely home to God. He suffered physical death, but he was raised to life in the Spirit.
>
> **1 Peter 3:18**

Today's reading is getting pretty long, so we'll pick it back up tomorrow. In the meantime, these are great verses to practice meditating on!

Week 06, Day 07

Learning the Gospel, Part 2

The blood of animals just wasn't cutting it...but, as we'll soon learn, the blood of animals was never intended to cut it. God, in His great love, chose to sacrifice Himself for our sins instead of allowing the constant sacrifice of animals for our sins.

> Just think how much more the blood of Christ will purify our consciences from sinful deeds so that we can worship the living God. For by the power of the eternal Spirit, Christ offered himself to God as a perfect sacrifice for our sins.
> **Hebrews 9:14**

The blood of Jesus Christ was infinite times more effective at solving humankind's sin problem than the blood of animals was.

> Under the old covenant, the priest stands and ministers before the altar day after day, offering the same sacrifices again and again, which can never take away sins. But our High Priest offered himself to God as a single sacrifice for sins, good for all time. Then he sat down in the place of honor at God's right hand.
> **Hebrews 10:11-12**

That perfect sacrifice is such good news! But, it's not automatic. The blood sacrifice that Jesus made left humankind with a choice.

4. Faith

The choice is simple: Will you place your faith (trust) in what Jesus did? Or won't you?

> God saved you by his grace when you believed. And you can't take credit for this; it is a gift from God. Salvation is not a reward for the good things we have done, so none of us can boast about it. For we are God's masterpiece. He has created us anew in Christ Jesus, so we can do the good things he planned for us long ago.
> **Ephesians 2:8-10**

"When you believed" is sometimes translated in the verse as "by faith." Faith is simply believing that Jesus is Who He says He is.

And not just simply believing (we talked about that before…even the demons believe), but actually choosing to follow Him.

When you choose to follow Jesus, the Bible tells us this:

> If you openly declare that Jesus is Lord and believe in your heart that God raised him from the dead, you will be saved. For it is by believing in your heart that you are made right with God, and it is by openly declaring your faith that you are saved. As the Scriptures tell us, "Anyone who trusts in him will never be disgraced."
>
> Jew and Gentile are the same in this respect. They have the same Lord, who gives generously to all who call on him. For "Everyone who calls on the name of the Lord will be saved."
> **Romans 10:9-13**

If you believe it and begin to live it out, the Bible says you will be saved! And did you notice that it said "Jew and Gentile are the same"? You might be wondering about that…Paul, the author of this passage, put that in there because some of the early Christians were racist (ring a bell?).

But God doesn't look at race. God looks at the heart. Because God is not a racist God.

Not only is God not racist, but in order for us to truly follow God, then that means we also must not be racist.

And then, going back to that Ephesians verse, it ends by saying that we were created as God's masterpiece!

You are a masterpiece! Handcrafted by the God of the universe!

And the purpose of you being a masterpiece is not simply so that you can look in the mirror and admire yourself…it's because He made you a masterpiece for a very specific purpose.

Jesus played a huge role in God's "Master Plan of Redemption!" But God also wants *you* to play a huge role in His Master Plan of Redemption! And that's what we'll spend our time on next week.

But for now, how are you doing with your meetups to discuss what you're reading? Are you able to do it regularly? Is it beneficial?

If you're not doing it, I recommend you find someone to do it with. Even if that means starting the book over. Seriously. You cannot underestimate the power and the growth potential that comes from reading through this stuff with someone else. Blessings!

Week 07

God's Master Plan of Redemption

In the beginning…and I mean all the way back to the beginning…that's where God's Master Plan of Redemption began.

You see, when God created the earth and everything in it, He looked down upon it and said that it was very good! And the place that He prepared for humankind to live was beyond very good…it was perfect.

God's instructions to Adam and his wife Eve were to tend to the garden. To help upkeep it (work is not always a bad thing), and to stay away from sin.

But…the devil disguised himself as a serpent, and he tempted Adam and Even in the garden. And that is when sin entered the world. And that's when humankind lost access to paradise, and a perfect, unhindered relationship with God.

At this moment, God turned to Satan, disguised as the serpent, and God said these words to him:

> And I will cause hostility between you and the woman,
>   and between your offspring and her offspring.
> He will strike your head,
>   and you will strike his heel.
> **Genesis 3:15**

That was perhaps the very first prophecy of what was to come.

And so for centuries and centuries, the OT describes story after story of humankind struggling with sin, and longing for a Savior. They knew that a Savior was on the way, but they just didn't know when.

> "The day is coming," says the Lord, "when I will make a new covenant with the people of Israel and Judah."
> **Jeremiah 31:31**

So the people waited…and they waited…and those who had faith were counted as righteous while they waited.

> Faith shows the reality of what we hope for; it is the evidence of things we cannot see. Through their faith, the people in days of old earned a good reputation.
> **Hebrews 11:11**

But when Jesus stepped onto the scene, He made the ultimate sacrifice and paid for the sins of humankind—once and for all for those who would believe!

Yet sin is paid for, and there is still pain. And there are still problems. And there are still weeds and thorns around that did not exist in the Garden of Eden. But that's because the plan isn't yet complete.

The plan is in motion, and Jesus has done His part…and now, there's another key player that God is looking to put into the game.

You.

God wants to use YOU to help carry out His Master Plan of Redemption!

> Because we understand our fearful responsibility to the Lord, we work hard to persuade others. God knows we are sincere, and I hope you know this, too…Either way,

Christ's love controls us. Since we believe that Christ died for all, we also believe that we have all died to our old life. He died for everyone so that those who receive his new life will no longer live for themselves. Instead, they will live for Christ, who died and was raised for them.

And all of this is a gift from God, who brought us back to himself through Christ. And God has given us this task of reconciling people to him. For God was in Christ, reconciling the world to himself, no longer counting people's sins against them. And he gave us this wonderful message of reconciliation. So we are Christ's ambassadors; God is making his appeal through us. We speak for Christ when we plead, "Come back to God!" For God made Christ, who never sinned, to be the offering for our sin, so that we could be made right with God through Christ.
2 Corinthians 5:11, 15-16, 18-21

God made you a masterpiece so that you can do some really good things that He planned for you a long, long time ago (see yesterday's reading). And part of what He planned for you was to use YOU to help carry out this task of reconciling people to Him, just as you have been reconciled to Him!

Reconciled (v): A big word that means making people who used to be enemies, friends (for more on that, go all the way back to Week 01, Day 02).

And that whole paradise thing that we lost, and a perfect relationship with God? Oh…that's still coming.

> The God of peace will soon crush Satan under your feet. May the grace of our Lord Jesus be with you.
> **Romans 16:20**

That day just isn't here yet.

But until that day comes, God is ready to put you in the game. He has uniquely created you as a masterpiece, and you are uniquely created in order to be able to reach some people for Jesus that nobody else can reach for Jesus!

Over the next few days, we're going to spend some time looking at how how uniquely God created you to be you, and how nobody else is created quite like you are.

You are a masterpiece. And God is ready for you to start doing what you were made for. Are you in?

CHANGED BY LOVE

Week 07, Day 02

Your Unique Design

You are a masterpiece. We've been over that already, but here's the thing about masterpieces that you may not realize—typically, there's only one.

Sure, copies will be made, prints, etc. But, think of Leonardo da Vinci's masterpiece, the Mona Lisa. There are prints all over the place. But as far as the *real* Mona Lisa, there is only one. And it is worth so much.

That is what God thinks of you! But, unlike the Mona Lisa, God's desire is not just for you to hang out in a museum and do nothing. God has uniquely designed you to do something that only you can do.

Let's revisit a verse from last week once more:

205

For we are God's masterpiece. He has created us anew in Christ Jesus, so we can do the good things he planned for us long ago.

Ephesians 2:10

God has big plans for you! And He's had these plans for quite some time. Nobody can fulfill these plans quite like you can!

And here is something that I think far too many American Christians fail to realize: God has equipped each and every one of us to be able to impact the world for His Kingdom! This is not something that He has just designated for pastors and priests. In fact, if we were to look at what the Bible says about priests, here is a verse you should keep tucked away in your memory bank:

And you are living stones that God is building into his spiritual temple. What's more, you are his holy priests. Through the mediation of Jesus Christ, you offer spiritual sacrifices that please God.

1 Peter 2:5

Did you catch that? God says that each and every woman and man who believes in Him should be operating as His holy priests!

That's what God thinks of you! The role of "pastor" or "minister" or "priest" or "missionary" should not be only reserved for people who have spent years in Bible college, and gone through an official ordination process. Those roles are reserved for people just like you!

God has already called you out as one of His followers. Now, God is calling you up to be one of His front women or men.

That is what God has designed you to be.

And I'm not just talking about someone who hands out bulletins at church (although the importance of that should never be diminished). I'm talking about somebody who can inspire real life-change in your community and beyond!

I came across a quote that is attributed to Saint Augustine, and I thought it was simply beautiful:

> "Men go abroad to wonder at the heights of mountains, at the huge waves of the sea, at the long courses of the rivers, at the vast compass of the ocean, at the circular motions of the stars, and they pass by themselves without wondering."

You're more important to God than the most majestic mountain! And God wants to use you to change the world!

The first step to being used by God, though, is to make a commitment to try. This is not something that will likely happen if you just sit back and wait. This is something that's going to take some willingness, and some "get up and go!"

As a follower of Jesus, you have been uniquely designed to fight against certain injustices. You have been uniquely designed to be able to reach certain people groups with the Good News. You have been uniquely designed to influence certain sectors of society that nobody else can influence quite like you can.

God created you to be the perfect person to reach those where you live, where you work, where you study, and where you play. And He's just waiting for you to tell Him you're ready.

God made you the way you are on purpose, and for a purpose.

> You made all the delicate, inner parts of my body
>   and knit me together in my mother's womb.
> Thank you for making me so wonderfully complex!
>   Your workmanship is marvelous—how well I know it.
> **Psalm 139:13-14**

Spend some time today thanking God for the way He uniquely designed you. Tell Him that you're ready for what's next!

Week 07, Day 03

Your Unique Wiring

What would you say if I tried to convince you that Jesus uniquely wired you to do similar things to the things that Jesus did while He was here on earth?

What would you say if I tried to convince you that Jesus uniquely wired you to do *even greater things* than the things that Jesus did while He was here on earth?

Well…I'm not going to try to convince you. I'll just let Jesus do the talking.

> "I tell you the truth, anyone who believes in me will do the same works I have done, and even greater works, because I am going to be with the Father." - Jesus
> **John 14:12**

Jesus has uniquely wired you, and other believers, to do some really great things for His Kingdom! But unfortunately, in America, I feel like we just leave the "great" things to be done for the Kingdom to the pastors and the missionaries.

God has uniquely wired YOU to do these things!

Now, timeout. Real talk. How does reading these things about yourself make you feel? Be honest. Does it make you nervous? Does it get you excited? …do you think I'm just crazy?

I want you to really grasp this, because I think this is important. I don't want you to settle for a bare minimum kind of life. God doesn't want you to settle for comfortable. God wants you to commit to real Kingdom-shaking kind of change!

Now you may be thinking that I don't really know you. That I don't know your story. That I don't know your shortcomings. That I don't know your limitations. And…you're right, I don't!

But God does.

> You watched me as I was being formed in utter seclusion,
>   as I was woven together in the dark of the womb.
> You saw me before I was born.

> Every day of my life was recorded in your book.
> Every moment was laid out
>   before a single day had passed.

Psalm 139:15-16

God knows you better than even you know you. And God has known you longer than you have known you. So, I'm going with God's opinion of you over your own opinion of you.

And if I've learned one thing from reading the Bible, it's that God sure does love a good underdog story!

So, back to your unique wiring. Only you and God can answer these questions for you, but think through these things:

1. Is there a certain cause or mission that really gets you excited, and moves you to action?

Maybe it's hungry children. Maybe it's victim advocacy. Maybe it's voting rights. Maybe it's those commercials you see on TV about starving animals. Maybe it's recycling, or mental health, or making knit hats for premature babies, or…fill in the blank.

What is something that, when mentioned, really gets your heart pumping? Something you could give a whole speech on without notes?

Take a few minutes to really think through that, and maybe jot down some possible answers.

2. What is a certain issue or injustice that really gets you fired up?

Maybe it's the mistreatment or underrepresentation of minority people groups. Maybe it's climate change. Maybe it's foster care. Maybe teaching English as a second language. Maybe it's resources for veterans.

Take a few minutes to really think through that, and maybe jot down some possible answers.

3. If you had a blank check from the world's richest individual with permission to spend as much money as needed, and you had an army of volunteers ready to help you accomplish one thing—what would that one thing be?

Solve world hunger? Eradicate pollution? Abolish country music? Cure cancer?

Take a few minutes to really think through that, and maybe jot down some possible answers.

Look over that list and adjust as needed. We are all on our way to finding out how God has uniquely wired each of us!

Week 07, Day 04

Your Unique Influences

In the United States of America, it seems like a lot of times American Christians get the Constitution our founding fathers wrote confused with the Bible that our Heavenly Father wrote. I hear people talk all the time about our constitutional freedoms, and they refer to them as our "God given rights."

These "God given rights" are typically things I don't really see mentioned or justified in the Bible. In fact, most of the characters we see in the Bible were not really "free" in the same ways that Americans are today.

But one thing that really bothers me is when I see Christians disrespect those around them while claiming to be Christ-like, and justifying it by saying that they are free.

I honestly think that one of the best ways we can truly demonstrate our freedom is by fighting for the freedom of those who aren't yet truly free.

Freedom should be less about me, and more about those who are still in bondage.

Typically, we see people who fight for the freedom of others labeled as "activists." Well, if that's the case, then it's safe to say that Jesus was the ultimate Activist.

Jesus did not consider his freedom as something worth fighting for, but instead, He fought for my freedom.

He fought for your freedom.

And so, as followers of Jesus, I think it only makes sense that you and I should be fighting for the freedom of those around us! And I don't think that this is a job simply for the pastor and the "professional Christians." I think this is a fight that we all have the privilege of joining in on!

> However, he has given each one of us a special gift through the generosity of Christ…Now these are the gifts Christ gave to the church: the apostles, the prophets,

the evangelists, and the pastors and teachers. Their responsibility is to equip God's people to do his work and build up the church, the body of Christ. This will continue until we all come to such unity in our faith and knowledge of God's Son that we will be mature in the Lord, measuring up to the full and complete standard of Christ.

Ephesians 4:7,11-13

Jesus gave gifts to His Church in the form of leaders, and in the form of certain kinds of influence. And the job of those with these gifts of influence is to build up the Church so that they can do God's work.

Jesus gave gifts to each of us. Jesus gave gifts to His Church. Do you know what that means? If you are part of the Church (people that follow Jesus), then that means that you have been given a special gift of influence!

For centuries, the American Church has acted as if this passage only means that pastors receive these gifts! But...read it again. That's not what it says!

It says these gifts were given to "each of us." So that means that you are included in the people who were given one of these gifts!

This list of gifts (Apostles, Prophets, Evangelists, Shepherds or Pastors, and Teachers) has been given the nickname "APEST." We will more fully explore the APEST gifts and what they mean in the next book, *Authentic Community*, but for now…know that YOU have been given one of these gifts!

And these gifts are to be used with those that you have influence with! So now…we need to ask the question: Who do you have influence with?

Here a few questions that you can use to really think this through:

1. Is there a certain people group that you really care about, and even get angry about when you see treated unjustly?

Maybe that people group is a certain ethnic group, say African Americans, or Hispanic Americans, or Asian Americans? Maybe it's Africans or Hispanics or Asians that are not Americans? Maybe it's Caucasian Americans?

Maybe it's orphans? Or kids in general? Or kids in single-parent homes? Maybe your heart really beats for single moms, or victims of domestic abuse, or maybe even single dads?

Take a few minutes to really think through that, and maybe jot down some possible answers.

2. What people group do you seem to simply have natural favor with?

Maybe it's people just like you. Maybe it's people radically different than you. Maybe it's sixty-something year-old women who enjoy coming together to knit blankets. Maybe it's high school rugby players.

Take a few minutes to really think through that, and maybe jot down some possible answers.

> Again Jesus said, "Peace be with you. As the Father has sent me, so I am sending you."
> **John 20:21**

As Christians, we have been "sent," just as Jesus has been sent. So, if you have been sent...

3. Who would you say you have been sent to? Who are "your people"?

Who really listens to you when you talk? Who follows you when you lead?

Maybe it has to do with the work you've done throughout your lifetime. Maybe it has to do with what you studied in school.

Maybe it has to do with the relationships that naturally form around you. Maybe it has to do with shared experiences you've had with a certain group of people.

Is there somebody that you just naturally get along with? Somebody that you can work really well together with, regardless of the project?

Take a few minutes to really think through those questions, and maybe jot down some possible answers.

When you are able to determine how God has uniquely given you influence, that will be the next step towards finding out the specifics of how you've been made into a masterpiece!

Take some time to pray over the questions from today.

Maybe even call somebody and ask them what they think. Maybe the answer you are looking for is being held by somebody that you have influence with!

Week 07, Day 05

Your Unique Gifts from God

This is probably one of my favorite topics to talk about, especially with followers of Jesus who have never before realized that they have been given unique gifts from God Himself!

> Now, dear brothers and sisters, regarding your question about the special abilities the Spirit gives us. I don't want you to misunderstand this.
> **1 Corinthians 12:1**

Even though Paul writes that he does not want us to misunderstand this, it seems like there is quite a bit of misunderstanding surrounding these "special abilities," or spiritual gifts that God has given to each and every believer—-including you!

Now, I have absolutely no idea how much you know about spiritual gifts. Maybe you're well versed in spiritual gifts. You know what yours are, you're actively practicing them, and you're even helping those around you discovery their spiritual gifts. Or…maybe this is the first time you're ever hearing about spiritual gifts.

Regardless of where you are, let's go on this journey together. Even if you've already studied all there is to study about spiritual gifts, perhaps today's reading will make you think about them in a fresh way!

First of all, let's define *what* spiritual gifts are. Spiritual gifts are abilities given to you that, before you were a follower of Jesus, did not come naturally to you. Sometimes the gifts might even seem "counterintuitive."

A good example is the gift of generosity. There are some people that I know that have the gift of generosity…but they really don't have a whole lot to give away. But regardless of how little they have to give away, they still seem to always be giving away what they have, and it always seems like the needs of their family are still taken care of.

That's an example of a gift that may seem "counterintuitive."

There are other gifts we've been given that we know of as "talents." These are gifts that we've always been good at.

A good example of a talent, or a natural gift, might be the gift of singing. There are some people that, even before they were a follower of Jesus, were just super good at singing! And they've always been good at singing! And now that they're a follower of Jesus, they're using that gift to lead others in worship.

Even though that gift is being used in a spiritual way, it is still not really a spiritual gift. It is a natural gift. A talent.

There are plenty of people who do not follow Jesus that have a natural talent for singing.

We're not going to get too in-depth with the entire list of spiritual gifts and all that they entail in today's reading. We'll take a deeper dive into spiritual gifts in the next book, *Authentic Community*, but for today, let's just cover a few basics.

One of the best ways I've discovered for people to start thinking about what their spiritual gifts may be is for them to take an assessment. Now, if you take an assessment, please remember that it's really hard to fit what God is doing in your life into a box. And most assessments are pretty much just that…a box.

While an assessment might be helpful to you in finding a general idea of what your gifts might be, don't take your test results as Gospel truth. It just might not be 100% accurate.

But then again, your results might just be spot on!

If you're ready to jump into a free spiritual gifts assessment, then feel free to navigate over to www.giftstest.com for a simple one.

Or if you're looking for a more in-depth analysis, then my friends over at Disciples Made have made a really great, free assessment that goes deeper: www.giftpassionstory.com

After you take an assessment and receive your results, be sure to pray about them. Reflect on them. Just because you might think they're correct does not mean that they are.

Just because you might think they're incorrect does not mean that they are, either.

Once you get your results, ask somebody close to you what they think about your results. Sometimes it's helpful to have input from someone close to us. They can see our blindspots.

Another good thing to do is to show your results to a mentor or a leader in your faith community or church, and ask them if there are some service projects that would be good for you to try, based on your results.

> In his grace, God has given us different gifts for doing certain things well. So if God has given you the ability to prophesy, speak out with as much faith as God has given you. If your gift is serving others, serve them well. If you are a teacher, teach well. If your gift is to encourage others, be encouraging. If it is giving, give generously. If God has given you leadership ability, take the responsibility seriously. And if you have a gift for showing kindness to others, do it gladly.
> **Romans 12:6-8**

This is not an exhaustive list, but I really like it because it really helps to drive home an important point about the ways that God has uniquely gifted you:

Your spiritual gifts are not given to you for your own gain.

> A spiritual gift is given to each of us so we can help each other.
> **1 Corinthians 12:7**

To God be the glory, the giver of all good gifts!

Week 07, Day 06

Your Unique Challenges

Today's topic about the unique challenges that we face will be especially hard for some people. So, I feel as if I need to give you a trigger warning for today's reading. We'll talk about the unique challenges that we've faced in our lives, and how God can use those for His glory, and for the growth of His Kingdom. But this might not be an easy conversation to have.

I know there are some people that have experienced terrible, traumatic, evil things in their lives…and some of these things have been recent. So, if you know that today is a day that you might not be able to handle…please skip today's reading and just go to tomorrow's reading. Or, just take today off. :)

Even if you lived an extremely sheltered life, I'm certain that you've still experienced struggles.

Here's what we're talking about today: What are some of the biggest struggles you've ever faced? What are the most difficult experiences you've dealt with?

Now, I understand that thinking through these things might be extremely hard to do…but thinking through them will be helpful in understanding how God has uniquely shaped you.

Maybe you had really painful experiences with your family, or a certain family member. Maybe you are a survivor of unthinkable abuse. Maybe for as long as you can remember, you've never had enough money to live a comfortable life. Maybe your struggles stem from a physical or mental disability.

I know that these things can be really hard to think through, but I really believe that God can use them for His glory.

Now…let me hit pause and say that God is a good, good God, and that God is not the one Who caused the pain in your life. Because that's not who God is.

The pain that we've all experienced is ultimately a byproduct of sin. The world that God created for mankind was pain free…but as humankind, we chose sin. And with the introduction of sin into our world came depravity.

The pain that we may have experienced at the hands of others is certainly an indicator of the depravity that we live in. It may be helpful to think about these things through the lens of "seasons."

As a child, I dealt with *this*… As a teenager, I dealt with *this*… As a college student, I dealt with *this*… and so on.

When you come up with a list of the difficult things you've experienced, whether that's a physical list or a mental list, then it's time to start thinking how the Lord can use the terrible, painful experiences for good.

Because we know that God likes to use all things for good.

> And we know that God causes everything to work together for the good of those who love God and are called according to his purpose for them.
> **Romans 8:28**

Once again, just a quick reminder that even if God allowed something to happen, that doesn't mean He caused it to happen.

But here's something that might be helpful to think through. When you were in the midst of your darkest days, was there somebody who was walking alongside you that had experience with what you were going through? Or were you all alone?

If you had somebody walk through it with you, then praise the Lord! You are very blessed that you did not have to walk through your darkest days alone.

But if you're like most people…I think you probably had to deal with those things alone. Whether you were afraid to share because of shame or threats, or you thought that people would judge you or not understand…oftentimes, we end up going through these experiences alone.

Now, imagine with me that you had somebody who had similar experiences, and they were willing to walk with you through your darkest night. Somebody who was able to say "I've been here… let me show you how God brought me through it."

Because of the unique challenges that you have gone through, God can use you to be that person to walk with somebody who is going though similar circumstances.

Pray about who might benefit from hearing some of your story.

Week 07, Day 07

Your Unique Purpose

Purpose (n): The reason for which someone exists.

Now that you've discovered your unique design, your unique wiring, your unique influences, your unique gifts, and your unique challenges, it's time to start discovering how God made you with a unique purpose.

And one of the best parts of having this discussion is, when you truly discover your unique purpose, it is something that you will absolutely love. It is something that you will be really excited about! It is something that you will want to share with others!

Finding your unique purpose in the world doesn't typically annoy people—it bring them incredible joy.

So now, we've got to ask a question. When you combine all the unique aspects of how you're created, how you're gifted, and what you've experienced...how can you use your unique shape and your unique story to impact the Kingdom?

Don't worry about trying to come up with something really big (but also don't shy away from coming up with something big)!

Think through the experiences that you've had, and what it would have meant (or did mean) to have somebody with similar experiences walk through them with you. Wouldn't that have meant the world to you? Even though it may have been considered "small" by the person walking through it with you?

If you could help even just one person get through the similar experiences that you've had, while you used your gifts and your influences to keep their eyes on God, that would be huge!

So what are you here for? How can you give God glory with your life? Why were you uniquely shaped the way that you were?

Author Mark Twain once said, "The two most important days in your life are the day you were born, and the day you find out why."

What a powerful quote! I have to say that I agree.

Why are you here? What did God make you to do?

The Lord was gracious to you, and you were able to find your way to Jesus and start following Him. Now, who else have you been uniquely shaped to help do the same?

What can you do to help better your community? What if your life and faith experiences are less about getting you to heaven when you die, and more about you helping get heaven to earth while you are still alive?

Jesus forgave us of our sins and brought us into His family not just so that we could experience freedom from shame and guilt, but so that we could help others experience freedom from shame and guilt as well!

As we grow more in our faith, we come to realize that our salvation is not just about saving us *from* something. We are also saved *for* a very specific purpose! No matter what we do, Jesus wants us to do it for the advancement of His Kingdom and of His glory!

Jesus want us to help other people grow in their faith.

> So whether you eat or drink, or whatever you do, do it all for the glory of God. Don't give offense to Jews or

Gentiles or the church of God. I, too, try to please everyone in everything I do. I don't just do what is best for me; I do what is best for others so that many may be saved. **1 Corinthians 10:31-33**

Do what is best for others.

If you truly live out your faith in this way, you will absolutely be living out your faith through your unique purpose!

As you live out your faith in this way, keep yourself in check by revisiting these two questions on a frequent basis:

1. **How can I continue to bring heaven to earth in my community?**

2. **How can I continue to bring heaven to earth in my church?**

What a great thing to discuss with your reading buddy this week!

To God be the glory!

Week 08

BLESS Rhythms

If I were to ask you, "At what point in Jesus' ministry did He hand over His authority with instructions to 'go'?", do you know if you would have an answer?

I've actually had this conversation with quite a few believers, some paid professionals (pastors, etc.), and some who are simply following Jesus for free. And when I ask the question, the number one answer that I get is the Great Commission—when Jesus was about to leave this earth, and this scene unfolded:

> Jesus came and told his disciples, "I have been given all authority in heaven and on earth. Therefore, go and make disciples of all the nations, baptizing them in the name of the Father and the Son and the Holy Spirit. Teach these new disciples to obey all the commands I have given you.

And be sure of this: I am with you always, even to the end of the age."
Matthew 28:18-20

While not everybody gives me that answer, the vast majority do. And because the vast majority of believers think that this is the case, it started being lived out in their faith communities and churches and in their ministries. The way that it plays out is that the "lead pastor" will hold on to power tightly, until it is their time to go. And when it is time for them to go, they then start looking around for a replacement. Yes, they look internally for a bit, until they realize that nobody within their ministry is qualified and equipped to lead, so then they start looking around for an outside hire.

But…what if I told you that Jesus gave His authority to His disciples long before He was about to leave? What if I showed you a passage where Jesus handed over His authority to ministry, even while He was "still in play"?

The Lord now chose seventy-two other disciples and sent them ahead in pairs to all the towns and places he planned to visit. These were his instructions to them: "The harvest is great, but the workers are few. So pray to the Lord who is in charge of the harvest; ask him to send more workers into his fields. Now go, and remember that I am sending you out as lambs among wolves.

"Whenever you enter someone's home, first say, 'May God's peace be on this house.' If those who live there are peaceful, the blessing will stand; if they are not, the blessing will return to you. Don't move around from home to home. Stay in one place, eating and drinking what they provide. Don't hesitate to accept hospitality, because those who work deserve their pay. "If you enter a town and it welcomes you, eat whatever is set before you. Heal the sick, and tell them, 'The Kingdom of God is near you now.'"
Luke 10:1-3, 5-9

Did you catch that? "Heal the sick and tell them about the Kingdom of God"?

Wasn't that Jesus' job?

Yes! It absolutely was! And Jesus was not planning on going anywhere anytime soon. In fact, as best as I can tell, this equipping and empowering and imparting of authority happened more than a year before Jesus was headed out...and in the grand scheme of things (a ministry that lasted a grand total of three years), a year is a really long time.

Jesus is way more interested in empowering the "normal, everyday Christian" to do great things for the Kingdom than He is in them just sitting back and watching the paid professionals get to have all the fun!

If we were to truly follow the example of Jesus, and how He equips and empowers those around Him, then our churches would *almost never* need to look outside their four walls for the next person to lead.

But…the "blame" for the way things are right now shouldn't only fall onto the shoulders of the pastors and the ministry leaders. The "normal, everyday Christians" are partly to blame as well.

Let me tell you why: If the "normal, everyday Christians" don't see themselves as Masterpieces made uniquely and on purpose for the good things that God planned for them to do long ago, then we will forever be stuck in the vicious cycle of only having "paid professionals" do it all.

That's a "top-down approach," and Jesus was not interested in it. Instead, Jesus is way more interested in a "bottom-up" strategy.

In that Luke 10 passage, did you notice how Jesus instructed His followers to enter into new relationships? He instructed them to lead with peace! Some other translations say "May God's blessings be on this house."

They were not instructed to go in yelling a "TURN OR BURN" message. Instead, they were instructed to go in with blessings, and with peace.

Over the next few days, I'm going to be sharing with you a tool called the BLESS Rhythms that was developed by my friend Dave Ferguson. These rhythms are based off of what he shares in his book, *BLESS: 5 Everyday Ways to Love Your Neighbor & Change the World.*

In addition to the rhythms developed by Dave Ferguson, I will be sharing a framework that I developed called the "BLESS Tracker," that makes actually practicing the BLESS Rhythms so simple that a child with no training at all could do them.

That's the goal. For every believer to realize that not only do they have the authority to "go ahead" and do ministry, but that they also have the know-how. Visit www.blesstracker.com for the most up to date information!

Are you ready? Let's go forward with peace, and BLESSINGS!

Week 08, Day 02

Begin with Prayer

If you haven't figured it out yet, BLESS is an acrostic—each letter stands for something. That why I keep capitalizing BLESS (I'm not just trying to yell at you). So maybe we could even write it out as B.L.E.S.S.

The "B" in BLESS stand for "Begin with Prayer." And while this may not seem like a big deal, it really is vitally important. First of all, because we need to remember Who's authority we are moving forward with (Jesus' authority), and second, because we need to remember that it is the Holy Spirit's job to draw people to Jesus.

The Early Church leader Paul framed sharing Jesus with others in a great way when he wrote this:

> After all, who is Apollos? Who is Paul? We are only God's servants through whom you believed the Good News.

Each of us did the work the Lord gave us. I (Paul) planted the seed in your hearts, and Apollos watered it, but it was God who made it grow. It's not important who does the planting, or who does the watering. What's important is that God makes the seed grow. The one who plants and the one who waters work together with the same purpose. And both will be rewarded for their own hard work. For we are both God's workers. And you are God's field. You are God's building.
1 Corinthians 3:5-9

You and I are only vessels, or tools, that the Holy Spirit uses to help bring people to Jesus (just like Paul and Apollos were just vessels or tools). We can plant and water all day long, but it is only God who can provide the growth. So…we begin with prayer.

Now, here comes the "BLESS Tracker" part:

When you determine a specific individual that you want to start sharing Jesus with through the BLESS rhythms, you should start praying for them, by name (if possible), in a very intentional way.

Now, keep in mind that you will probably get to the point where you are praying for more than one individual, and that's great! But I'd love to encourage you to spend, at the very least, 60 seconds in focused prayer for each individual that you are trying to BLESS, per day. At least. So realistically, you probably want to keep your focused BLESS list to somewhere between 5-8 people.

Pray for God to use you as a vessel to bless them. Pray that the Lord would stir up good questions about the Christian faith in their heart. Pray that they would feel comfortable asking you some of their questions. Pray that the Lord would grant you favor in their lives.

When you have spent some intentional time in prayer for a specific individual, give yourself one point.

> +1 | I intentionally prayed for _____.

If you have the chance to naturally (not forcefully) mention to an individual that you are praying for them, then that is the next (optional) step in the "BLESS Tracker."

Imagine that you are spending time with this individual, even if it is just a quick interaction. And imagine if you were able to say something along the lines of: "I don't know if this means anything to you or not, but I am a praying person. This afternoon when I pray, is there anything that I can be praying for you about?"

I have never seen anybody get offended by that approach. Ever.

Typically, even people who do not believe in prayer at all will say "No, I'm ok." But then the next time you ask the question, they open up about something that they're going through. They might even tell you that they are flattered that you would spend time praying for them!

So, if the person you are trying to BLESS gives you a prayer request, then give yourself two points (and be sure to pray for the prayer request)!

+2 | _____ gave me a prayer request.

After you do this a few times, there might be a time when the individual you are trying to BLESS approaches you and, uninitiated, asks for prayer! And if that happens, that is a huge step in the right direction! If they say something like, "I know you're a praying person, will you pray for me in this way?", that should be celebrated by giving yourself three points!

+3 | _____, uninitiated, asked me for prayer.

Once you get into the rhythm of practicing the BLESS Rhythm of beginning with prayer...STAY THERE!

If you remember the Luke 10 passage from yesterday when Jesus gave His authority to His followers and sent them out, here were some of His specific instructions:

> Don't move around from home to home. Stay in one place, eating and drinking what they provide. Don't hesitate to accept hospitality, because those who work deserve their pay.
> **Luke 10:7**

So keep praying for this one individual.

And stay there.

And if the Lord provides a unique opportunity to jump ahead to another part of the BLESS Rhythms, then by all means, take that opportunity! But if the Lord does not move early, give yourself permission to "stay there" for awhile.

And, unless the Lord moves in another way, stay at the B in BLESS until you get to the point where you have "ten points" with the person you are trying to BLESS!

When you get to ten points, it's time to be brave! Let's move into the next phase of the BLESS Rhythms!

Week 08, Day 03

Listen and Engage

When we are practicing the BLESS Rhythms using the "BLESS Tracker," one thing we need to be very careful not to do is put God in a box. The tracker is a little box, and God doesn't fit too well in little boxes. And so, with that in mind, think of this tracker as more of a "framework" in which you can work.

Even better, maybe you can even think of this Tracker framework as a trellis.

If you're anything like me, I just lost you.

A trellis is one of those criss-cross looking things that vines grow really well on. Sometimes you'll see them in people's backyards, lining a fence that has a vine growing on it. Or…somewhere else that a trellis and vine would look nice. I don't know. I'm not the right guy to teach you about trellises (and I have no idea if that's the plural of trellis). But what I do know is that Jesus said this:

> Yes, I am the vine; you are the branches. Those who remain in me, and I in them, will produce much fruit. For apart from me you can do nothing.
> **Luke 10:7**

What I've found is that vines are hard to contain (and God is not able to be contained), but a trellis does a really good job of giving the vine a really good place to go.

Instead of a box, think of this "BLESS Tracker" as a trellis on which Jesus, the True Vine, can grow in your life as you aim to BLESS those around you!

So, you've gotten to "ten points" with the person you are trying to BLESS, and now it's time to move into the "L" part of BLESS: Listen and Engage!

Listening is an art form, and I think that there are fewer and fewer of those artists remaining. Think of the last time that somebody *really* listened to you, without allowing themselves to be distracted by their phone, or by somebody else passing by, or by their watch, or their phone, or their phone, or their phone...

When you get a chance, really, really listen to the person that you are trying to BLESS. Ask them questions about themselves. Ask them about their experiences. Ask them about their story.

Sometimes, I literally sit down with somebody and say, "So, tell me something interesting about you!" And, typically, they are caught off guard by that. Because they've never been asked that before. But…I've never had anybody tell me that they don't a single interesting thing to share about themselves!

Everybody has a something to share.

When you get to the point where you can really listen to the person you are trying to BLESS without being distracted by the millions of different distractions around you, you will start to really learn some things about that person.

But don't expect them to be really deep things. Superficial things are ok at this point in the "BLESS Tracker!"

When you get to the point where you learn something new about the individual you are trying to BLESS by listening to them (not through gossip), then give yourself a point!

+1 | I learned something new about _____.

Learning simple facts about individuals really is a powerful thing. And it certainly makes people feel loved to know that they are starting to be known. Even if there are things that I learn about somebody that I really could care less about, it's good for me to get to know the person I am trying to BLESS.

But if I am able to learn about a common shared interest by listening to them, then that is what I would consider a breakthrough! If you are able to find (by listening, not by gossip) a common interest that you share with the individual you are trying to BLESS, give yourself two points!

> +2 | I found a common interest with _____.

Common interests really are powerful things! And they don't even have to be deep! It could literally just be a shared hobby, or a taste in music, or a certain kind of food (it's amazing how many people share a common interest for fine cheese!), or it could be a certain cause that you are both passionate about.

Whatever it ends up being, common interests are powerful.

And then, when you have a chance to act on something that you learned about that individual (by listening), then that is something that is worth three points!

> +3 | I acted on something I learned about _____.

Now, you may be wondering what I mean by "acted on." What does that mean, exactly?

It's simple, really. It's learning that your friend collects postcards, and picking one up for them the next time you go somewhere interesting. It's learning that your friend really likes flowers, so you invite them to go with you to the Flower Festival that you're going to next week. It's learning that they really like cheese, and giving them a hot tip on a really good new cheese that you found and love and is on sale right now!

When somebody sees that you are truly listening to what they are saying, and that you truly care enough to act on something you've learned by listening to them, then that is a really powerful thing. It begins to tear down walls of separation that people naturally build up around themselves.

And when they see that you really care, chances are, they will start to care back.

Now, keep in mind that the prayer points and listening points are starting to compound at this point! Don't stop praying! But when you get to twenty-five points, move on to the next step!

Week 08, Day 04

Eat Together

Do you remember when I described this "BLESS Tracker" tool as a box? Well, here is a great example. Oftentimes, eating together and listening go hand-in-hand. Not always, but often.

And so if you find that the Lord is opening up the opportunity to eat together (or get coffee, etc.) with the individual that you are trying to BLESS before you have twenty-five points, then by all means, do it!

We cannot control the Vine!

But if the Lord doesn't move in a unique way before you get to twenty-five points, then by all means wait to move to this step until you've stayed at the other steps for awhile.

Another disclaimer that I should mention is that I am viewing this step (and all steps) through the lens of my current location, which is Vancouver, WA, in the Pacific Northwest. Originally, I am from Tennessee, and the points system, especially for this step, might look just a little bit different in Tennessee that they do in Washington State.

But I trust that you can take the idea and adjust it to your context as needed. After all, nobody is uniquely designed to reach the people around you better than you! You are God's masterpiece! I trust that you know what you're doing! :)

The first point in this step comes when I find a chance to go out somewhere to eat or get coffee with the individuals that I am trying to BLESS.

> +1 | I went out to eat/got coffee with _____.

Now keep in mind that these points are still compounding. So be sure to intentionally pray for the individual you are trying to BLESS by name before you meet up, and also be sure to try and earn some "listening points" as well while you are together. This could move from one point to quite a few pretty quick, if you are intentional with it!

As you continue to grow in your relationship, pray for this individual, and listen and engage, there might be a time where it is natural for you to invite them over to your place for a meal or for some coffee! If you are able to actually host them for a meal, etc., then give yourself two points!

+2 | I was able to host _____ for a meal/coffee.

Especially in the Pacific Northwest, there is a certain level of trust and *platonic* intimacy (Jesus is not your dating wingman) that comes along with going over to someone's house for a meal.

So if you get to the point where the individual that you are trying to BLESS actually invites you over to their place for a meal and/ or coffee, then that is when you can give yourself thee points!

+3 | _____ hosted me for a meal/coffee.

Especially in the culture I am currently in, this is such a huge deal. Like...it doesn't happen without a serious level of trust. It really is a rarity.

But going back to the conversation that I was having a minute ago, this is something that might need to be adjusted according to what culture you are currently in. Because "Southern Hospitality" is not just a cute saying...it is a real thing that actually exists. And Pacific Northwesterners might not believe this, but there have been times when I've met somebody for the very first time in the South, and they've said, "Well why don't y'all come over for supper tonight?"

Let me be clear…that is not a three pointer!

The point system in this "BLESS Tracker" tool is designed to reflect levels of platonic intimacy and trust that go both ways, and sometimes, in different cultures, you have to find creative ways to earn that platonic intimacy and trust in your given context.

But that's why Jesus sent you to where you are, and why Jesus sent me to where I am! I'm uniquely designed to reach people in Vancouver, WA. You are uniquely designed to reach people where God has called you to be!

You are not where you are by accident. Instead, you have been sent there on purpose, and for a purpose!

Hopefully by now, you are really starting to see points compound in a "snowball effect" kind of way! As you pick up speed with these BLESS rhythms, hopefully you are starting to really gain momentum with the individuals you are trying to BLESS! Now, when you get to forty points, let's move to the next step!

Week 08, Day 05

Serve

Earlier in this book, we talked about how we have true freedom in Christ, and how true freedom really comes through the ability to lead others to true freedom as well.

But don't just take my word for it, let's see what Paul has to say!

> For you have been called to live in freedom, my brothers and sisters. But don't use your freedom to satisfy your sinful nature. Instead, use your freedom to serve one another in love. For the whole law can be summed up in this one command: "Love your neighbor as yourself."
> **Galatians 5:13-14**

Your freedom is really not about you. Your freedom is about others, and your ability to love and serve them well!

Assuming you've gotten to the point on your "BLESS Tracker" where you have forty points (or assuming the Vine is growing in ways not planned, and opening doors of opportunity that you are stepping through in obedience), then it is time to move to the next part of the BLESS Rhythms!

If you find an opportunity to serve them in a meaningful way, then give yourself one point!

> +1 | I found a meaningful way to serve _____.

One thing that I've found is that when you begin to selflessly serve people the way that Jesus did, you really, really, really begin to stand out from the crowd! In a world that is so selfish, self-centered, and individualistic…serving people in meaningful ways really tends to turn some heads.

Now, as you begin to serve, and as people begin to turn their heads, feel free to jump around to the final rhythm if you feel it is appropriate, especially if they ask you good questions.

We should never have the end goal of drawing more attention to ourselves by serving people. Instead, we want to take the eyes that are pointed our way, and direct them to the One who is worth paying attention to!

Now, who will want to harm you if you are eager to do good? But even if you suffer for doing what is right, God will reward you for it. So don't worry or be afraid of their threats. Instead, you must worship Christ as Lord of your life. And if someone asks about your hope as a believer, always be ready to explain it.

1 Peter 3:13-15

If you are eager to do good, people will start to notice. In a good way. And when they ask you about why you are serving so well, always be ready to give an answer. And remember, the answer is never that you are simply a good person (remember that Bible verse that says "none are righteous"?)! It's because the One that you ultimately serve is good, and He gives you the hope that you have within you!

If you continue this behavior, then before long, this kind of behavior may be reciprocated! And if you ever get to the point where they do something to serve you in a meaningful way…give yourself another two points!

+2 | _____ served me.

If they truly find a way to serve you, that is really them showing some intentionality on their end! That means that you are someone that has significance in their lives! That means that you are really starting to earn their trust! Praise God for the unique influence that He has given you with this person! Now, see if you can use that influence to move to the next step of both of you serving somebody else, together! If you get to that place where the individual that you are trying to BLESS is working alongside you to help BLESS somebody else, then that is worth a well-earned three points!

> +3 | _____ and I served somebody else together.

There is something really special and bond-building (and barrier breaking) about serving somebody together. For instance, have you ever done service projects with other people in your faith community? Maybe even done a mission project or mission trip together? If you think back to that time, you'll probably recall that serving together made your relationship with that other person stronger than it was before.

The same thing can and will happen when you serve together with the individual that you are trying to BLESS!

With all of these points compounding together, it won't be long at all before you get to sixty points! And sixty points is when you should move into the next rhythm, if you're not already there!

Week 08, Day 06

Story

If you're to the point where you have sixty points in the "BLESS Tracker" with a single individual, then there is a good chance that you may have already done some of this stuff, especially in the "Listen and Engage" part, or maybe over coffee or a meal when you were in the "Eat Together" stage of the BLESS Rhythms.

The first step here is to share deeper, meaningful parts of your story with the individual you are trying to BLESS. If you are able to do that, then give yourself one point!

> +1 | I shared parts of my story with _____.

The key here being deeper and meaningful. It's ok to talk about your love for cheese, but the point here is to talk more about struggles that you've endured, or pain you've experienced.

What are parts of your unique story that have shaped you into who you are today? If you're comfortable with it, share some of the unique challenges you've experienced in your life.

When you lead with vulnerability and authenticity, those things go a really long way.

It seems like the world that we live in today is one where we are only accustomed to touting our strengths, talents and abilities.

Try sharing about something significant you tried to do in your life…and then failed at. How did that make you feel? What did you learn from it?

I guarantee that if you do this, you will be well on your way to getting them to share some deeper, more meaningful parts of their story with you. And when that happens, it's time to give yourself another two points on your "BLESS Tracker!"

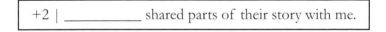

+2 | _____ shared parts of their story with me.

Again, the key here is deeper and more meaningful.

Sometimes, I literally sit down with somebody and say, "So, tell me your story!" And, typically, they are caught off guard by that. Because they've never been asked that before. But, do you know that I've never had anybody tell me that they don't have a story?

Everybody has a story.

And, if they are being vulnerable and authentic with you, please, please, PLEASE do not be looking at your phone! Because there's no quicker way to throw a wet blanket on that fire than to do that.

As you listen to deeper parts of their story, and maybe even things that they've struggled with, then that is a great way to start piecing together the missing pieces to a highly relevant "three circles" conversation! And if that happens, you will be at the point where you are having a meaningful Gospel conversation with your friend! If that happens, add another three points to your "BLESS Tracker!"

> +3 | I had a Gospel conversation with _____.

The key here is "conversation," as opposed to "presentation." A lot of times, Gospel presentations are forced or unnatural, and they sometimes come across as unauthentic. With the level of relationship you now have with the individual that you are trying to BLESS, a Gospel conversation should maybe even be natural at this point!

If you need a refresher on how to have a "three circles" conversation, take a second to flip back to Week 02, Day 03 through Day 06. It's a lot to re-read in one sitting, but maybe you can practice drawing the "three circles" design and filling in the blanks over the next few days.

If you feel like a "three circles" conversation is not up your alley, or maybe it doesn't feel "right" for the individual that you are attempting to BLESS, then maybe you could give them their very own copy of the *Curious?* book that precedes this one in the "Curious to Kingdom Multiplier" series!

And…oops! I just showed you my cards.

Part of what I believe God has called me to do is to help you become a "Kingdom Multiplier!" And you're not the only one… the person that you're working on BLESSing…let's turn them into a Kingdom Multiplier as well! :)

Back to the conversation for today. If you begin a Gospel conversation, and it seems like your friend is disinterested, that's ok. There will hopefully be a time soon when you can try again.

You've made it this far! Let's not do anything to lose the relationship, if we can help it! Keep pushing towards the goal!

Keep praying, listening, eating, and serving!

Week 08, Day 07

Shaking the BLESSed Dust Off

We began this week by talking about how Jesus gave His authority to those who were following Him, He sent them out to places that they were uniquely shaped to reach, and then told them to "stay there" as long as they were being received.

But then that begs the question…how long were they instructed to "stay there"? And more importantly, with the people that we are attempting to BLESS, how long should we "stay there" if they don't seem to be very receptive of what we're trying to share with them?

Well, let's revisit that passage together, and see if Jesus gave us any instructions on when to stop "staying there," and to "move on," instead.

Don't move around from home to home. Stay in one place, eating and drinking what they provide. Don't hesitate to accept hospitality, because those who work deserve their pay…But if a town refuses to welcome you, go out into its streets and say, "We wipe even the dust of your town from our feet to show that we have abandoned you to your fate. And know this—the Kingdom of God is near!"

Luke 10:7, 10-11

There comes a point where we are instructed to brush the dust off of our feet and move on.

How do we know when that time comes?

To those that are using the "BLESS Tracker" tool, my suggestion is to "stay there" with an individual until you reach 100 points with that one individual.

There will be times when that means you've made it through every single BLESS Rhythm on the chart, and just can't seem to move any further. There will be other times when you have not been able to move past the very first step…but in that case, that means that you will have intentionally prayed for that individual, by name (if possible) no less than 100 times!

That's pretty powerful.

If you get to the place where you have 100 points with a single individual, nobody is going to ever look at you and say that you didn't try.

You did try. In fact, you tried very well. And that is very respectable.

But there will be times when you've reached 100 points with an individual, and you do NOT want to move on! And do you know what I think? I think that's even better!

Stay there!

You never know what the Lord can do with somebody who is stubbornly faithful in trying to BLESS somebody!

Stay there!

Allow me to share something powerful that can happen if you start using this "BLESS Tracker," and how powerful it is to not just do it by yourself, but to do it with others who are in your faith community or church.

The "BLESS Tracker" introduces a common language that can be used among you and others who are also aiming at BLESSing their family, friends, and neighbors!

Imagine with me that you ask your friend, who is also a follower of Jesus, how they are doing on their "BLESS Tracker." Imagine with me that they say, "I'm at an 87 with one of the individuals I am trying to BLESS! And I just added a new individual to my BLESS list, and I am at a four with them!"

All of the sudden, you have a real framework for knowing exactly where that person is, and how you can pray for the individuals that they are trying to BLESS!

Not only does that add an element of accountability and collaboration through prayer, but they can also join you in celebrating and praying about where you are on your "BLESS Trackers!"

And who knows…maybe that will even encourage others to take their "BLESS Trackers" a little more seriously or maybe even to try harder!

A little healthy competition never hurt anyone! :)

Happy BLESSing! Don't forget to visit www.blesstracker.com for the most up to date information!

Week 09

The Armor of God

One thing that we must be aware of is that when we begin to work towards the expansion of the Kingdom of God, and when we work towards doing our part to bring Heaven to earth, then we will be making some very real enemies.

Yes, there will be other people who fight against what you're doing (even though I never really fully understand why people would fight against their community being a better place to live). But the very real enemies that I'm talking about are not other people.

That early Church leader, the Apostle Paul, was very familiar with opposition. He experienced opposition from many people, but he knew that his real enemy was not other humans. He understood that his enemies were the leaders of the kingdom of darkness.

A final word: Be strong in the Lord and in his mighty power. Put on all of God's armor so that you will be able to stand firm against all strategies of the devil. For we are not fighting against flesh-and-blood enemies, but against evil rulers and authorities of the unseen world, against mighty powers in this dark world, and against evil spirits in the heavenly places.
Ephesians 6:10-12

This is what Paul wrote to the Church in Ephesus, as they were striving to do some really good things in their community. Paul was not naive enough to think that their effort would not be opposed, and he wanted to share with them how they could protect themselves well against the enemy.

And I am hoping the same thing for you. That as you begin to work at bringing Heaven to earth, and as you start BLESSing those around you, that you would know how to protect yourself against attacks from the enemy.

Paul continues:

Therefore, put on every piece of God's armor so you will be able to resist the enemy in the time of evil. Then after the battle you will still be standing firm. Stand your ground, putting on the belt of truth and the body armor of God's righteousness. For shoes, put on the peace that comes from the Good News so that you will be fully prepared. In addition to all of these, hold up the shield of faith to stop the fiery arrows of the devil. Put on salvation as your helmet, and take the sword of the Spirit, which is the word of God.

Pray in the Spirit at all times and on every occasion. Stay alert and be persistent in your prayers for all believers everywhere.
Ephesians 6:13-18

Over the next few days, we will unpack the individual pieces of armor together, why they are important, and what they mean for you as a follower of Jesus. But, before we jump in to talking about them, there is something that I want to point out.

Belt...body armor...shoes...shield...helmet...those things are all built for defense (I guess a belt could go both ways). When we put on the armor of God, we will be very well protected against attacks from the enemy. But there's something else in that list:

A sword!

As follower of Jesus, you and I are not called to just sit back and play defense. Jesus has a desire for us to play offense as well. And when the Church goes on offense while Jesus rides shotgun, the Church is unstoppable (I said "while Jesus rides shotgun, because I mean about things that Jesus cares about…I'm not talking about when people in the Church get offended by coffee cups)!

Side note: There is a big difference between going on the offensive against the powers of the kingdom of darkness, and being offensive.

We are not called to be a people that are offensive to our fellow Image Bearers of God.

> Do all that you can to live in peace with everyone.
> **Romans 12:18**

Those are pretty simple instructions!

Tomorrow, we will talk more about the implications of the Armor of God. But for now, rest in the fact that God has a plan to protect you as you do your part.

He not only gave you a jersey…but pads, as well! :)

Week 09, Day 02

The Armor of God, Part 2

Yesterday, we ended with talking about the need to not be offensive. I think that another thing we need to keep watch for is how easily we are offended.

There was a time, about 1,700 years ago, when there was no place on earth where a government gave freedoms to Christians. And when the Christians were living as outlaws, they only had time to really focus on the things that mattered.

There were less divisions among believers, because they didn't have time to argue and bicker over trivial matters. Even simply gathering together to pray or eat together was risky business, because they faced the prospect of being arrested—or something much worse—for their faith.

That changed in the Roman Empire in the year AD 312 as the Roman Emperor, Constantine, made Christianity the official religion of the Roman Empire. The Christians in Rome that had been facing persecution as the minority culture suddenly found themselves in the majority culture, and they no longer had to worry about their fear of persecution.

So, majority culture Christians, with the favor of their government, began arguing over trivial matters and their preferences instead of ways to combat the kingdom of darkness.

When soldiers get too comfortable in enemy territory, things don't seem to end well. And that is why Paul wrote this to his primary disciple, Timothy:

> Soldiers don't get tied up in the affairs of civilian life, for then they cannot please the officer who enlisted them.
> **2 Timothy 2:4**

When Christians get caught up in being offended because their preferences are being overlooked, that is the same as soldiers getting tied up in civilian affairs. Instead, you and I must stay focused on a mission that matters.

When we stay focused on what matters, we will be unstoppable.

Listen to what Jesus Himself said would happen when the Church plays offense for things that matter:

> Now I say to you that you are Peter (which means 'rock'), and upon this rock I will build my church, and all the powers of hell will not conquer it.
> **Matthew 16:18**

Typically, I love the New Living Translation (NLT) of the Bible, because it's simple to understand and fairly accurate. But this is one instance where I do not prefer the NLT.

Most translations don't say "the powers of hell will not conquer it," but instead say something along the lines of "the gates of hell will not be able to stop it."

Gates instead of power. Stop, instead of conquer.

Let me explain to you why I think it's important that we make this distinction. "Power & conquer" sound like words that are most often associated with offense...so if I've got mostly defensive equipment, and I'm going to war against the power of hell that are trying to conquer...that gives me the impression that we're going to lose.

However, "gates & stop" sound like words that are most often associated with defense...so if I've got a sword, and I'm going to war against the gates of hell that are attempting to stop us…that gives me the impression that we're going to win!

The NT was originally written in mostly Greek, and the original Greek word that was used here is "πύλη" (pronounced "poo-lay"). This is the Greek word for "gate."

Going back to Ephesians 6…we've got plenty of defense, and we are equipped for offense, but there is one more thing that we cannot forget about—our intel and our coms (short for intelligence and communications systems).

Let's revisit the last verse of that Ephesians 6 passage once more so that you can see what I mean by coms:

> Pray in the Spirit at all times and on every occasion. Stay alert and be persistent in your prayers for all believers everywhere.
> **Ephesians 6:18**

When coms systems break down, soldiers are left alone to fend for themselves. But if we stay connected to our commanding officer through prayer, He promises that He will never leave us! He will be with us always, until the end of times!

Week 09, Day 03

The Helmet of Salvation

Starting from the top, we are instructed to "put on salvation as our helmet." A helmet has one job. Whether we're talking about a medieval knight or a toddler riding a tricycle, a helmet protects your head.

There are many parts of your body that you could do without, but your head is not one of them.

I recently took a tumble down a flight of stairs that left me pretty banged up. When my wife got to her poor, whimpering husband at the bottom of the stairs, the first thing she asked me was, "did you hit your head?"

She convinced me to go to Urgent Care to make sure there were no broken bones, etc. When I got to Urgent Care and explained what happened, the first thing the intake nurse asked me was, "Did you hit your head?" The triage nurse got to the room and asked, "Did you hit your head?" When the doctor got it, he asked "Did you hit your head?"

Although I had not hit my head, I was beginning to wonder if my behavior was giving them a reason to ask me if I had hit my head! But...that wasn't it. They were simply concerned that the most vulnerable part of my body, which I could not do without, had been injured.

Without our salvation, there is no hope.

But because we have our salvation—and our assurance of that salvation—we know that the most vulnerable and important part of us is protected. We who live in the light of Jesus can be unafraid to combat the darkness. Whether we are stepping into the darkness to try and do our part to bring heaven to earth, or we are actively working to BLESS those around us, we should have no fear.

> But let us who live in the light be clearheaded, protected by the armor of faith and love, and wearing as our helmet the confidence of our salvation.
> **1 Thessalonians 5:8**

When we put on our helmet of salvation and step into the darkness to fight for justice, we do not go alone. Even if we are physically alone in a particular instance, we are not alone in the fight. The Lord has gone before us, and He will be with us.

He has been putting on the helmet of salvation and fighting for justice for thousands of years!

> ...The Lord looked and was displeased to find there was no justice. He was amazed to see that no one intervened to help the oppressed. So he himself stepped in to save them with his strong arm, and his justice sustained him. He put on righteousness as his body armor and placed the helmet of salvation on his head. He clothed himself with a robe of vengeance and wrapped himself in a cloak of divine passion.
> **Isaiah 59:15b-17**

The Lord was very displeased to find nobody fighting for justice, or intervening to help the oppressed...may that never be said of our generation!

Instead, may our generation be full of brave women and men who have decided to follow Jesus with their lives, and have decided to not keep their salvations to themselves, but to bravely follow Jesus into the darkness to fight for justice. May our generation go out into the darkness to feed the hungry, clothe the naked, welcome the immigrant, and give water to the thirsty…all in the name of Jesus!

May our generation be known for the way we continuously aim to BLESS those around us, and then hopefully teach them how to BLESS others, after they choose to follow Jesus.

May our generation be known for going into the darkness, without fear, because we know that we are equipped with the Helmet of Salvation, and that there is nothing the enemy can do to snatch that helmet away from us!

> And I am convinced that nothing can ever separate us from God's love. Neither death nor life, neither angels nor demons, neither our fears for today nor our worries about tomorrow—not even the powers of hell can separate us from God's love. No power in the sky above or in the earth below—indeed, nothing in all creation will ever be able to separate us from the love of God that is revealed in Christ Jesus our Lord.
> **Romans 8:38-39**

Let us go forward with boldness!

Week 09, Day 04

The Body Armor of Righteousness

Next up is the "Body Armor of Righteousness," oftentimes referred to as the "Breastplate of Righteousness." When we become followers of Jesus, we have the ability to put this spiritual body armor on. You might be thinking, "But if this body armor comes from our righteousness, then wasn't I able to put this on when I did good things, even before I was a follower of Jesus?

The Bible is clear on that very question:

> We are all infected and impure with sin. When we display our righteous deeds, they are nothing but filthy rags. Like autumn leaves, we wither and fall, and our sins sweep us away like the wind.
> **Isaiah 64:6**

We did not have access to this spiritual body armor because of the sin problem that plagued us all.

> For everyone has sinned; we all fall short of God's glorious standard.
> **Romans 3:23**

Even when we were doing the best work we've ever done, our "righteousness," or good deeds, had no way of outweighing the sin debt that we owed.

> As the Scriptures say, "No one is righteous— not even one. No one is truly wise; no one is seeking God. All have turned away; all have become useless. No one does good, not a single one."
> **Romans 3:10-12**

Now, when that above verse says that "no one does good," it doesn't mean that nobody has ever done a good deed. That would be ridiculous. Even apart from followers of Jesus, I know of some people doing some really good things. In fact, some of the people who do the "most good" in our community do not identify as Christians (we really need to change that by US doing better). This verse means something different. It's talking about people doing good by God's standard. We don't meet it.

That is, we don't meet God's standard of good apart from Jesus (for more on this idea, revisit Week 06, Day 06).

But when you and I became followers of Jesus, Jesus literally gave us access to His righteousness. This is an idea known among scholars as "imputed righteousness."

Have you every heard the phrase "guilty by association"? Well, this Theological term known as "imputed righteousness" basically means just the opposite: "righteous by association with Jesus."

> When people work, their wages are not a gift, but something they have earned. But people are counted as righteous, not because of their work, but because of their faith in God who forgives sinners. David also spoke of this when he described the happiness of those who are declared righteous without working for it:
>
> "Oh, what joy for those
>   whose disobedience is forgiven,
>   whose sins are put out of sight.
> Yes, what joy for those
>   whose record the Lord has cleared of sin."
> **Romans 4:4-8**

And so with that imputed righteousness that we get from following Jesus, He transforms us into a new creation.

> So we have stopped evaluating others from a human point of view. At one time we thought of Christ merely from a human point of view. How differently we know him now! This means that anyone who belongs to Christ has become a new person. The old life is gone; a new life has begun!
> **2 Corinthians 5:16-17**

The righteousness that we receive by being associated with Jesus then becomes the spiritual body armor that you and I have the ability to wear. And with this spiritual body armor of righteousness, you and I have the ability to stand our ground in the fight.

But remember, it is not automatic. We must choose to make this decision daily (similar being filled with the Spirit).

> Instead, clothe yourself with the presence of the Lord Jesus Christ. And don't let yourself think about ways to indulge your evil desires.
> **Romans 13:14**

Week 09, Day 05

The Shield of Faith

Faith is something that you and I can never take for granted. It is of the utmost importance. Faith, although sometimes really small, has the power to do some really big things!

> The apostles said to the Lord, "Show us how to increase our faith." The Lord answered, "If you had faith even as small as a mustard seed, you could say to this mulberry tree, 'May you be uprooted and be planted in the sea,' and it would obey you!'"
> **Luke 17:5-6**

Faith has the ability to be a real game-changer in our lives. And although this previous verse makes faith look like an offensive measure (sometimes it is), in this list of armor, it is defensive. It is faith that acts as our spiritual shields.

> In addition to all of these, hold up the shield of faith to stop the fiery arrows of the devil.
> **Ephesians 6:16**

Now, if you've watched any movies or tv shows that depict medieval battles, chances are you've seen fiery arrows being shot at the opposing army in order for the arrow to not only pierce the skin on the opponent, but to sear into their body, and maybe even catch them on fire.

Now, as terrifying as that sounds, that is not something that the devil has the ability to do to us, if we belong to Jesus. Don't get me wrong, the devil's intent is to destroy, but Jesus has rescued us from the grip of the devil.

> For he has rescued us from the kingdom of darkness and transferred us into the Kingdom of his dear Son, who purchased our freedom and forgave our sins.
> **Colossians 1:13-14**

So, if we've already been rescued from the kingdom of darkness, and the fiery arrows of the enemy are unable to do to us what happens in the movies, then what is the point of the fiery arrows?

Simple. To distract us.

In medieval battles, fiery arrows were actually not used the same way that Hollywood depicts them being used. Instead, the primary use of fiery arrows was to set fire to structures around them.

You see, the enemy knows that if you are engaged in battle, but your world is on fire, that will be a major distraction to you. If a group of soldiers break off from fighting the enemy to go fight a fire instead, that very seriously diminishes the effectiveness of that army.

The purpose of the Shield of Faith is not so much to keep the enemy's arrows out of yourself (Jesus has got that covered). The primary purpose of the shield of faith is to eliminate the distractions around you.

If the devil cannot neutralize you (he cannot), then he will instead aim to make you ineffective through distractions. And here's the deal about distractions...sometimes they don't always look bad on the surface (think about the legalization of Christianity that led to Christian in-fighting as mentioned just a few days ago (Week 09, Day 02).

That was a major distraction that caused Christians who now enjoy majority culture to take their eyes off the goal.

But if we put our minds (and faith) to it, I think we can get back to doing battle with our shield of faith by eliminating the distractions that have neutered the Church in America for centuries.

> What good is it, dear brothers and sisters, if you say you have faith but don't show it by your actions? Can that kind of faith save anyone? Suppose you see a brother or sister who has no food or clothing, and you say, "Good-bye and have a good day; stay warm and eat well"—but then you don't give that person any food or clothing. What good does that do?
>
> So you see, faith by itself isn't enough. Unless it produces good deeds, it is dead and useless.
>
> Now someone may argue, "Some people have faith; others have good deeds." But I say, "How can you show me your faith if you don't have good deeds? I will show you my faith by my good deeds."
>
> You say you have faith, for you believe that there is one God. Good for you! Even the demons believe this, and they tremble in terror. How foolish! Can't you see that faith without good deeds is useless?
> **James 2:14-20**

Week 09, Day 06

The Belt of Truth & Shoes of Peace

I chose to combine the Belt of Truth and the Shoes of Peace because both ultimately have to do with mobility (shoes allow you to move around quicker, and it's hard to move around with your war pants around your ankles)! Also, both Truth and Peace should go hand-in-hand, even though it may look like sometimes Truth and Peace are on opposite ends of the spectrum.

If Truth is peanut butter, Peace is jelly. Too much jelly, and the sandwich is far too sweet. Too much peanut butter, and the sandwich is also undesirable. But equal parts of each go really, really well together!

Sometimes, it is necessary to speak Truth that is not easy to speak, but if your speech is seasoned with grace, love, and peace, then there is a much higher likelihood that it will be received in a way that will lead to action.

Let's begin with the Belt of Truth. If you don't have a belt, your britches will sag too much for you to be an effective soldier for Jesus. If you don't speak the truth, you will not go far.

Do you know somebody who often struggles with the truth? Sure, they may gain a brief following with their "alternative facts," but ultimately, they are not somebody who can be trusted.

They are not somebody that people will follow long-term.

> The very essence of your words is truth;
>   all your just regulations will stand forever.
> **Psalm 119:160**

The Words of God are Truth. Therefore, the words of God's people should also reflect Truth.

> Jesus said to the people who believed in him, "You are truly my disciples if you remain faithful to my teachings. And you will know the truth, and the truth will set you free."
> **John 8:31-32**

As followers of Jesus, you and I must wake up everyday and put on the Belt of Truth. A great way to do that is to begin your day with Truth (by spending time talking with God and reading His Word). Then, make a commitment to sharing Truth with those you encounter throughout your day.

And then…let's get our shoes on!

> For shoes, put on the peace that comes from the Good News so that you will be fully prepared.
> **Ephesians 6:15**

Now, there are plenty of different sources of peace, but not all kinds of peace are equal. For instance, the peace you get from eating a brownie ("peace, my dudes!") does not come anywhere close to the peace that comes from following Jesus.

The Peace we are supposed to put on is the Peace that comes from the Truth of the Good News (or the Gospel) of Jesus!

> Don't worry about anything; instead, pray about everything. Tell God what you need, and thank him for all he has done. Then you will experience God's peace, which exceeds anything we can understand. His peace will guard your hearts and minds as you live in Christ Jesus.
> **Philippians 4:6-7**

Do not worry about anything!

Before Jesus physically left the earth, He turned to His followers, and He said this:

> I am leaving you with a gift—peace of mind and heart. And the peace I give is a gift the world cannot give. So don't be troubled or afraid.
> **John 14:27**

Just because you have been given a gift, that doesn't mean it is automatically put to use. You have to actually engage with the gift you've been given.

I'm reminded of how my 3 year old son who is obsessed with construction vehicles and construction tools begged and begged me to get him a jackhammer. So, on his 4th birthday, we gave him a jackhammer (which I now understand is the opposite of peace in our household). And when the gift was brand new, he walked around the house constantly with that jackhammer. You couldn't pry that thing out of his hands if you tried!

But now that the newness is worn off, the jackhammer just lays on the floor, unused. And while my wife and I aren't too disappointed in the fact that it's not constantly used anymore (because now there is more peace in our house), we are reminded that we should not treat the gifts that Jesus gives us with the same apathy we treat the gifts we receive from others.

There are many people who claim to follow Jesus who no longer seem to be operating from a position of Peace. Perhaps when Jesus first gave them the gift of Peace, they played with it every single day...maybe there was nothing anybody could to pry God's peace out of their hands!

But now...the gift of Peace that Jesus gave them has been forgotten about. It just lays there on the floor, and goes unused.

> Therefore, since we have been made right in God's sight by faith, we have peace with God because of what Jesus Christ our Lord has done for us. Because of our faith, Christ has brought us into this place of undeserved privilege where we now stand, and we confidently and joyfully look forward to sharing God's glory.
> **Romans 5:1-2**

Friends, do not allow yourself to forget the gift of Peace that Jesus has given us. And "not forgetting" is not enough. Let's not forget to put it on daily!

Don't be caught barefoot in the battle!

Week 09, Day 07

The Sword of The Spirit

Put on salvation as your helmet, and take the sword of the Spirit, which is the word of God.
Ephesians 6:17

Swords were used by soldiers as both defensive and offensive weapons. With the right training, not only could a soldier use a sword to eliminate an enemy, but a soldier could also use a sword to protect themselves.

But regardless of if the sword was used primarily for offense or for defense, the fact remains that extensive training was required with the sword before it was most effective.

As believers, you and I must also undergo extensive training with our sword, in order for it to be the most effective in our spiritual lives, both offensively and defensively.

But a big difference between an actual sword, and the Sword of the Spirit which is the Word of God is this…the sword we have access to is alive!

If you're like me, the first thing your mind goes to is the "singing sword" from the classic Looney Tunes animation, "Knighty Knight Bugs" (1958)! But…thankfully, the sword we've been equipped with cannot be outdone by the wits of Bugs Bunny or Yosemite Sam!

> For the word of God is alive and powerful. It is sharper than the sharpest two-edged sword, cutting between soul and spirit, between joint and marrow.
>
> It exposes our innermost thoughts and desires. Nothing in all creation is hidden from God. Everything is naked and exposed before his eyes, and he is the one to whom we are accountable.
> **Hebrews 4:12-13**

The Sword that we have by our side is alive and powerful! And one of the beautiful things about that is, it doesn't entirely depend on us!

The Word of God is powerful enough to stand on its own, even when we don't know what to do or say.

> But when you are arrested and stand trial, don't worry in advance about what to say. Just say what God tells you at that time, for it is not you who will be speaking, but the Holy Spirit.
> **Mark 13:11**

But just because the Word of God is alive and can stand on its own does not mean that you and I should not train. We should. For it is the power of the Word of God itself, combined with our extensive training, that makes it most effective.

Give the most powerful weapon in the world to somebody who has zero training, and you're sure to see nothing but destruction.

> Work hard so you can present yourself to God and receive his approval. Be a good worker, one who does not need to be ashamed and who correctly explains the word of truth. Avoid worthless, foolish talk that only leads to more godless behavior.
> **2 Timothy 2:15-16**

Now, I know that all this talk of "working hard" and "extensive training" may sound daunting. You may even be asking yourself, "But how do I properly train with the Sword of the Spirit?"

Well…I've got some good news for you!

Chances are, if you've made it this far into this book, then you are already actively training with the Sword that the Spirit has given to you! If you've already been actively involved in Bible study, both group study and personal Bible study like we talk about in Week 03, Days 04-07 (and elsewhere in this book), then you have already been training!

Moving forward, my hope is that this training with your Sword that is active and powerful will continue! Maybe your training will even increase in intentionality, now that you understand more about how important it is to both offense and defense!

> We are human, but we don't wage war as humans do. We use God's mighty weapons, not worldly weapons, to knock down the strongholds of human reasoning and to destroy false arguments. We destroy every proud obstacle that keeps people from knowing God. We capture their rebellious thoughts and teach them to obey Christ.
> **2 Corinthians 10:3-5**

As believers, you and I are in a very real spiritual battle. And God wants you on the front lines. Stay trained up!

Week 10

Fruits of The Spirit & Love

So I say, let the Holy Spirit guide your lives. Then you won't be doing what your sinful nature craves. The sinful nature wants to do evil, which is just the opposite of what the Spirit wants. And the Spirit gives us desires that are the opposite of what the sinful nature desires. These two forces are constantly fighting each other, so you are not free to carry out your good intentions. But when you are directed by the Spirit, you are not under obligation to the law of Moses.

But the Holy Spirit produces this kind of fruit in our lives: love, joy, peace, patience, kindness, goodness, faithfulness, gentleness, and self-control. There is no law against these things!

Galatians 5:16-18, 22-23

When we become Christians, Jesus tells us that His Holy Spirit comes and lives within us (see Week 01, Days 03 & 04, as well as Week 04, Day 04). And when the Spirit comes to live within us, He comes bearing gifts (see Week 07, Day 05), but He also helps us as Jesus followers to live a life that is defined by some really good fruit!

Just like a tree is defined by its fruit, so should you and I as Jesus followers be defined by our fruit!

> You can identify them by their fruit, that is, by the way they act. Can you pick grapes from thornbushes, or figs from thistles? A good tree produces good fruit, and a bad tree produces bad fruit. A good tree can't produce bad fruit, and a bad tree can't produce good fruit. So every tree that does not produce good fruit is chopped down and thrown into the fire. Yes, just as you can identify a tree by its fruit, so you can identify people by their actions. **Matthew 7:16-20**

The very first fruit that we as followers of Jesus should produce in our lives is love! Love is not only where it starts, but love should be a defining feature of our lives. But one thing that is important to remember about the fruits that the Spirit produces in our lives is…they're from the Holy Spirit! They're not from us!

It's not that, all of the sudden, we are capable to start producing these fruits in our lives once we start following Jesus. Instead, seeing evidence of these fruits is how we can determine that the Spirit is active and working and moving through somebody.

The fruit is not from me. The fruit is from the Holy Spirit.

> As the Scriptures say,
> "No one is righteous—
>   not even one."
> **Romans 3:10**

Now, when discussing "love" in the context of the Bible's Fruit of the Spirit, it's important to understand that our modern day interpretation may not always mean the same thing.

I love cheese. But that love is from me, not necessarily the Spirit.

The word "love" used in this instance in the Bible is a word that can be transliterated as "Agape" (ah-gah-pay). Because in the Greek (the language that some of the Bible was originally written in), the word "agape" means so much more than the kind of love that I can have for cheese.

I love cheese, but I wouldn't die for it (even though my wife is convinced that I might die *from* some of the cheeses I enjoy).

Agape love is an unconditional love. A love that forgives. A love that always assumes the best. A love that is unoffendable.

Check out how the Bible describes this kind of Agape love:

> Love is patient and kind. Love is not jealous or boastful or proud or rude. It does not demand its own way. It is not irritable, and it keeps no record of being wronged. It does not rejoice about injustice but rejoices whenever the truth wins out. Love never gives up, never loses faith, is always hopeful, and endures through every circumstance.
> **1 Corinthians 13:4-7**

When I read about that kind of love, I know that it is a love that I am not capable of by myself. But when I live my life in step with the Spirit of God, then this is a kind of love that people around me experience.

Love like this is a testimony of God's grace!

Week 10, Day 02

Joy & Peace

In the original language of the Bible, there is a Greek word called "Charis" (Kare-iss) that means "grace," or "gift," or "favor." For example, this word was used when the angel came to Mary and announced that she would be giving birth to Jesus.

> "Don't be afraid, Mary," the angel told her, "for you have found favor with God!"
> **Luke 1:30**

The Greek word for "joy" in the Bible is the word called "Chara" (Kaw-raw). The idea is that Chara is the natural response to Charis. When we received the favor of God through His Holy Spirit, He brought about a true and lasting joy in our lives!

Our joy comes from living in the love that Jesus has for us as His followers, and behaving in the way that Jesus wants us to (which I hope, by now, you understand is not just following a list of rules)!

> I have loved you even as the Father has loved me. Remain in my love. When you obey my commandments, you remain in my love, just as I obey my Father's commandments and remain in his love. I have told you these things so that you will be filled with my joy. Yes, your joy will overflow!
> **John 15:9-11**

When we live our lives with the love that Jesus want us to live with, and when we live like Jesus did by obeying His commands, then we will be filled with overflowing joy! What an incredible promise!

Not only do we have the opportunity to live our lives with great joy through the Holy Spirit, but we can also live our lives with great peace. And not just any peace, but a peace so peaceful that it doesn't even make sense to those around us!

> Don't worry about anything; instead, pray about everything. Tell God what you need, and thank him for all he has done. Then you will experience God's peace,

which exceeds anything we can understand. His peace will guard your hearts and minds as you live in Christ Jesus.
Philippians 4:6-7

A peace that exceeds anything we can understand. That's a pretty serious kind of peace. And while the Greek words are not directly related, it seems that the Greek word for peace, "Eirene" (i-ray-nay), is similar to the idea of reconciliation.

Reconciliation is the act of two enemy parties becoming friends. It's a relationships that "exceeds anything we can understand."

Therefore, since we have been made right in God's sight by faith, we have peace with God because of what Jesus Christ our Lord has done for us. Because of our faith, Christ has brought us into this place of undeserved privilege where we now stand, and we confidently and joyfully look forward to sharing God's glory.
Romans 5:1-2

The peace that we as sinners have with a holy God because of something He did for us (instead of what we do for Him) "doesn't make sense." It is something beyond anything we can understand. And that peace shouldn't just stay within ourselves (peace is something that is usually thought of as an internal

2

attribute), and it is not just something between us and God…but it is something that should also extend between us and other people!

> Never pay back evil with more evil. Do things in such a way that everyone can see you are honorable. Do all that you can to live in peace with everyone.
> **Romans 12:17-18**

In a world that seeks revenge when wronged, Jesus calls us to extend forgiveness to those who wrong us, and to live in peace with them.

And that is a peace that exceeds anything human reasoning can make sense of. Remember, this is what Jesus told us we should say when we pray:

> Pray like this: Our Father in heaven, may your name be kept holy…and forgive us our sins, as we have forgiven those who sin against us.
> **Matthew 6:9, 12**

If somebody were to look at your day-to-day, would "joy" and "peace" come to mind? If not…is there something you can do to more intentionally live in The Spirit?

Week 10, Day 03

Patience & Kindness

Dear brothers and sisters, be patient as you wait for the Lord's return. Consider the farmers who patiently wait for the rains in the fall and in the spring. They eagerly look for the valuable harvest to ripen. You, too, must be patient. Take courage, for the coming of the Lord is near. **James 5:7-9**

There are some translations of the Bible that use the word "long-suffering" instead of "patience," especially when referring to the fruit of the Spirit. I think that "long-suffering" is a really strong translation to what the Bible is really talking about.

Patience is an important thing for us as believers to have because…well, let's just be honest: there are certain experiences, certain circumstances, and certain people that require quite a bit of long-suffering in order to deal with them. But when we deal with difficult things with great patience, it is pleasing to God!

One of the more difficult things about patience is that it's not often fun. There are some fruits of the Spirit that are just fun (who doesn't love being known for their love and joy)! This is not one of them. But when we are able to endure hard things with patience, it really sends a strong message to those around us who are watching us.

We may have to go through difficult times without knowing when they will end, and in these moments it can be tempting to lose our temper, or to give up, or to become bitter…but patience allows us to persevere through these challenges while we trust in God's timing.

Patience is also important in our relationships with others. It helps us to be understanding and compassionate towards others, even when they make mistakes or behave in ways that frustrate us. By being patient with others, we can show love and kindness in a way that helps build and strengthen our relationships.

Acting with patience is not always easy. It 's not natural. It requires us to rely on God.

It may mean we need to intentionally set aside our own desires and plans in order to wait on God's leading. It may also mean seeking out opportunities to intentionally practice patience, such as volunteering to help others with tedious tasks, or taking on projects that require a lot of time and effort.

Ultimately, patience is a fruit of the Spirit that comes from a heart that is rooted in faith and trust in God. It is a reflection of God's character and his loving, patient nature. As we seek to grow in patience, we can pray for the Holy Spirit to produce this fruit in our lives and ask for His strength and guidance as we strive to be patient in all things.

As you're practicing patience, it can help us to be more kind to those around us…which is very convenient since the next fruit of the Spirit is just that: Kindness!

> But the Holy Spirit produces this kind of fruit in our lives: love, joy, peace, patience, kindness, goodness, faithfulness, gentleness, and self-control. There is no law against these things!
> **Galatians 5:22-23**

Kindness is an important characteristic to be mindful of, as it allows us to show compassion and concern for others in a way that reflects the love of God.

One way to think about kindness versus simply "being nice" is that kindness is a willingness to do good things for others without expecting anything from them in return. It involves a selflessness that puts the needs and well-being of others before our own.

This can take many simple forms, such as offering a listening ear to a friend in need, helping someone with a task they are struggling with (that may require you flexing your patience muscle), or simply showing an act of kindness towards a stranger.

Kindness is also often characterized by a generous spirit and a willingness to give time and resources to help others. This could involve donating time or money to a worthy cause, volunteering to serve others in need, or simply being there for someone when they need support.

Kindness is not only shown through our outward actions, but it also involves an internal compassion and/or empathy towards others. It means being able to see the circumstances through other people's eyes, and being compelled to act in a way that would help meets their needs. This kind of internal change requires us to set aside our own wants, our own desires, and our own ego in order to focus on the needs of others.

Kindness, unlike patience, can be a fun one! But, just because it can be fun doesn't mean it's easy. This is especially true in a world that often emphasizes self-centeredness and competition.

A true, Spirit-filled kindness requires us to be intentional in our actions and to choose to put others first. It requires us to love our neighbors as ourselves. It also requires us to rely on the strength and grace of the Holy Spirit, as we seek to reflect His love and compassion in the world.

As we strive to grow in kindness, we can pray for the Holy Spirit to produce this fruit in our lives, and ask for His guidance and strength as we seek to be a source of kindness and compassion to those around us.

What is a way that you can be intentional about practicing both patience and kindness today? Or this week?

Who is somebody in your life that most embodies these fruits of the Spirit? Why don't you schedule some time with them?

Ask them what their secret is! See if you can learn their ways!

Week 10, Day 04

Goodness & Faithfulness

Goodness, a quality that refers to doing what is right regardless of the consequences, is characterized by honesty, generosity, compassion, and a genuine desire to help others. In the context of the fruits of the Spirit, goodness refers to the act of doing good not just to others, but being good to yourself as well.

Even though the fruits of goodness and kindness are often used interchangeably, they are distinct from each other. They are absolutely different.

Goodness is about doing good for others, being good to yourself, and doing good for God.

Kindness, on the other hand, refers to the act of being gentle, compassionate, and considerate towards others. It involves being understanding and forgiving. It involves being merciful. It is about being caring and understanding towards others, and making an effort to help and make their lives better.

If kindness is like mercy (not getting the bad things that we deserve), then goodness is like grace (receiving good things that we have not earned).

While both of these fruits of the Spirit involve doing good things for yourself and others, they are different in the "type" of good that is done.

Goodness focuses on doing what is right.

Kindness focuses on doing what is compassionate.

Goodness might even be more task-oriented, while kindness may be considered more people-oriented.

Bottom line: both goodness and kindness reflect the character of a God that loves us dearly, and a God who wants us as His followers to be known for our love.

This only makes sense, as we, followers of the one true God, have been changed by His love.

In order for us to live our lives marked by Goodness, it requires us to have a heart that actually desires good. And we know that, apart from God, our hearts aren't really all that good.

> The human heart is the most deceitful of all things, and desperately wicked. Who really knows how bad it is?
> **Jeremiah 17:9**

Faithfulness refers to being somebody who is reliable, dependable, and loyal—not simply in your relationship to others, but also in what you believe, how you act, and in your faithfulness to God.

Faithfulness means keeping your promises, acting with consistency, and being a trustworthy kind of person.

This is something that really is possible with God, even though it goes so much against our human nature.

In order to live a life that is marked by faithfulness, we must first be faithful in what we believe (and Who we believe in). It's ok to learn, to grow, and to change when we realize an error in our ways…but there are things that, in order to remain faithful, we should not mix with our Christian faith.

Things like crystals, tarot cards, and manifestation…while these things are all popular things to believe in (or at the very least dabble in), these things do not reflect a lifestyle that is faithful to the way of Jesus.

Being faithful means not being flip-floppy. And dabbling in the things listed above while claiming to follow Jesus is a pretty flip-floppy thing to do.

Faithfulness also means being the friend that will always be there, no matter what. The friend that will be there when times are really hard.

The 3:00am phone call.

Faithfulness also refers to being faithful, not just in your beliefs and with your friends, but with your loved ones and with God as well.

Being faithful with your loved ones means putting their needs above your own, even when it's inconvenient.

Being faithful to God means being mindful of trying to be obedient to what He has asked you to do, whether that ask is something specific (a particular calling), or general (a command found written out in the Bible).

Much like goodness and kindness are closely related, so are goodness and faithfulness. These fruits don't just complement each other, they complete each other.

It's hard to be good without being faithful.

It's hard to be faithful without being good.

Now, it's important to remember that these things, being fruits of the Spirit, are not simply talents and characteristics that are present within us…but they are attributes of God that we have the privilege of imitating now that we are followers of Jesus!

When we strive to be marked by both goodness and kindness, it leads us to experience a more full life that is evidenced by the presence of God in our lives.

Not only do these things make us more fun to be around, but they make us more accurately reflect the true Image of God in our lives.

Now, close this book for today, and go be good and faithful!

Week 10, Day 05

Gentleness & Self-Control

Gentleness refers to a demeanor or behavior that is mild, soft, and gentle. It is characterized by a kind and compassionate nature, a willingness to listen, and a non-judgmental attitude towards others.

In the context of the fruits of the Spirit, gentleness refers to treating others with kindness, compassion, and understanding, even in difficult circumstances.

To live with gentleness, you must first develop a heart that is kind and compassionate. This means making an effort to understand others, listen to their concerns, and show empathy.

It also means making an effort to control your emotions and reactions, avoiding anger, frustration, and judgment towards other people.

Understand this, my dear brothers and sisters:
You must all be quick to listen, slow to speak, and slow to
get angry. Human anger does not produce the
righteousness God desires.
James 1:19-20

Also, you must be willing to work towards forgiving people, even
when it is difficult, and to show compassion and understanding.

Self-control, on the other hand, refers to the ability to control
your own thoughts, emotions, and actions. It carries with it the
idea of being disciplined, and having the ability to master your
own impulses and make deliberate, conscious choices that reflect
your values and goals (whether those values and goals are spoken
or unspoken).

In the context of the fruits of the Spirit, self-control refers to
having mastery over your own desires, control over yourself
through the temptations that come your way, and the ability to
make choices that honor God and reflect your commitment to
follow Him.

A person without self-control
is like a city with broken-down walls.
Proverbs 25:28

To live out self-control, it helps to first be aware of your own desires, temptations, and weaknesses. Self-awareness is key. This means being honest with yourself about what you struggle with, and seeking the help of others and God when necessary.

> As iron sharpens iron,
> so a friend sharpens a friend.
> **Proverbs 27:17**

Practically speaking, the next step is to establish boundaries and rules for yourself, and to make a conscious effort to follow them. This means setting aside time for prayer and reflection on God's Word, avoiding things that are tempting or harmful, and making choices that reflect your values and goals.

Finally, a good way to grow in self-control is by developing good habits and discipline. This means making an effort to grow in the spiritual disciplines such as prayer, Bible study, and participating in a local church community.

> Don't you realize that in a race everyone runs, but only one person gets the prize? So run to win! All athletes are disciplined in their training. They do it to win a prize that will fade away, but we do it for an eternal prize. So I run with purpose in every step. I am not just shadowboxing. I

discipline my body like an athlete, training it to do what it should. Otherwise, I fear that after preaching to others I myself might be disqualified.

1 Corinthians 9:24-27

Gentleness and self-control are very closely related, and they complement each other well. Gentleness without self-control can lead to indecisiveness and a lack of direction, while self-control without gentleness can lead to harshness and a lack of compassion.

To live out these fruits of the Spirit effectively, you must strive for both gentleness and self-control, seeking to cultivate a heart that is kind and compassionate, while also being disciplined and in control of your thoughts, emotions, and actions.

The fruits of gentleness and self-control are essential qualities for all believers, and are enabled in our lives by following Jesus. These fruits involve us treating others with kindness and compassion, while also having a mastery over our own thoughts, emotions, and actions.

By striving to live out these qualities, we can experience the fullness of God's presence in our lives, and we can work to bring glory to His name with our lives!

Week 10, Day 06

Looking Back

Wow…we've covered SO MUCH GROUND in this book! I hope that you didn't take this journey alone, and that you were able to process this stuff with somebody else.

We talked about our salvation in Christ, what it means to be a part of the family, and the security that comes in knowing whose we are…but we also talked about the important of living like it, and the importance of things like baptism.

We then explored easy and impactful ways to engage in faith-filled conversation with those around us. Things such as asking someone about the best thing that ever happened to them and actually listening well to their answer…thus building trust and leading to deeper conversations. And we talked about doing service projects together!

Another idea was to make a list of friends you would like to share with and to start praying for them, and to be intentional in your "third places" such as coffee shops or bars, and to listen to the conversations around you.

We also talked about the idea of always staying prayed up and ready to share about the hope that is within you.

Then, we talked about best practices for prayer (both private prayer and group prayer), as well as Bible study (both private Bible study, and group Bible study).

We also spent some time discussing the Holy Trinity and the implications of our belief in a God that is Three in One, as well as how to wrap our minds around the Kingdom of God and how to bring heaven to earth.

In hindsight…that was probably too much to cram into a single week. Oopsie! :)

And then we got to one of my favorite "weeks" that we spent in this book…and that is the "Imago Dei!" We talked about what it means for us to be created in the Image of God, and how we can most fully live that out including (but not limited to) becoming more like Jesus with our heads, hearts, hands, and habits!

Any time that we get to move information from our noggins to our fingers and toes, I get pretty excited about it! Hopefully, that excitement has been passed down to you as well!

After that, we got to spend some time discussing the marching orders that Jesus left for His followers before He left this earth— The Great Commission. We talked about how to walk that out, how to make disciples, how to be disciples, and then we talked about how to read the Bible and understand its different genres.

We had the opportunity to also take a deep-ish dive into what the Gospel actually is, and how the Gospel should inform how we live our lives.

After that, we talked about God's "Master Plan," and how He wants to use YOU to carry out that plan! We talked about all the different ways that God created you to be incredibly unique, so that you can reach your part of the world in ways that only YOU are equipped to do!

I don't know about you, but just thinking through this stuff is incredible humbling and honoring to me! God thought so highly of you and me, that He created us with special skillsets, experiences, and personalities, so that we can reach our friends like nobody else in the world is equipped to do! Wow!

And then we spent some time talking about the BLESS Framework, as taught by my friends Dave and Jon Ferguson, and then I introduced you to a tool that I have developed called "BLESS Tracker."

I hope that this tool will be beneficial to you as you try and share your faith with your friends in a real and authentic way!

Finally…we spent an entire week (or maybe longer?) discussing the Armor of God, and then another whole week talking about the fruits of the Spirit.

And then…we're here.

Congratulations…you now know just as much as some guy who self-published a book!

But here is where I want to remind you, once again, about that whole "head, heart, hands, and habits" thing. If all you do with this knowledge is keep it stored away in your head, it will change nothing. It won't even make you that smart (in order to do that, you would need to read a book written by somebody smarter than me)!

Before you move on to tomorrow, I encourage you to take a few minutes to think about ways you can actually start living this stuff out!

Week 10, Day 07

What's Next

In my last book, *Curious? Everything you need to make an Informed decision about Jesus,* I made a promise to you. At the risk of going to plagiarism jail, here is that promise copied and pasted:

> I want to invite you into life with a much bigger purpose. And here's my promise to you: I will do everything in my power to help you get to that life with a much bigger purpose![1]

If you're a follower of Jesus, then that means Jesus is probably a big part of your life (or at least, you're trying for Him to be). And here's the deal about Jesus...Jesus is love.

And when you start following Jesus, Jesus changes you.

---

[1] If you're reading this footnote, then you can't sue me for plagiarism.

That is precisely why this book that you're holding in your hands (or that a robot is reading to you...thanks, future) is called *Changed By Love*.

The goal is for this to be book number 2 in a 5 book series, and each one of these books aims to help you move closer to living a life with a much bigger purpose.

Book 3 is going to be called *Authentic Community*.

In book 3, we will explore even more about what it means to live life in a community of people who are truly seeking the real Jesus, and living their lives for the purpose of love.

After that is book 4, *Life-Changing Experiences*.

When we live our lives for Jesus, He will change our lives in some pretty radical ways. He leads us to do things and go places that some people only dream of.

And this new life we have the privilege of living for Jesus is for something much bigger than ourselves...it is all for love. It is all for Jesus!

Finally, book 5 is *Life On Purpose*.

You already know the purpose. Love.

Jesus.

The Kingdom of God.

In book 5, we will walk through some incredible opportunities together, and take some huge strides toward living our lives for the purpose of love.

We might even end up changing the world on the way!

So, if you've made it this far...there's one question that remains:

Are you ready to keep going?

Are you ready to find out exactly what it means to experience authentic community so that you can also have life-changing experiences, and a life on purpose?

If you're ready, let's go!

But wait...before you run off...don't forget about the "Thresholds" section at the end of this book (as in, the very next page).

Before you move on to book 3, it really will be helpful to you to try and cross everything off of that checklist found in the "Thresholds" section.

Remember that our relationship with Jesus should never feel like a "checklist" kind of faith…but sorry.

This book has a checklist.

But even if you never even do the first thing on the checklist, Jesus still loves you. And I could probably still be talked into at least grabbing coffee with you (TBD on the "I still love you" thing).

But seriously…it's for your own good. :)

And like I said at the beginning of this book and way too many times in the last book, I cannot wait to take the next step of this journey with you!

I hope to see you over in book 3!

Much love!

Thresholds

Threshold [thre-ˌshōld] noun:
the place or point of entering or beginning

At the end of each of these books, I will have a list of "thresholds" that are good to pass though/do before moving onto the next book. Basically… "graduation points."

Make sense?

Moving on to the next book won't really make a whole lot of sense until you've finished the thresholds at the end of the previous book.

▓ Start living a Spirit-filled life.

▓ Get baptized.

▓ Share your story (testimony).

▓ Start a list of pre-Christians to start praying for.

▓ Discover your Unique Gifts.

▓ Lead Somebody Through the *Curious?* book (which is equivalent to discipling them!).

▓ Begin being discipled by a Christian you know and trust.

▓ Practice using the "Bless Tracker."

▓ Practice "putting on" the Armor of God.

▓ Be intentional in living a life marked by the fruits of the Spirit.

▓ Buy the next book…go on! Do it!

Whenever you get to the point in your life when you can put a checkmark in those boxes, then it's time to move on to book 3!

Authentic Community.

If you need help finding it, you know what to do… :)

360.836.0639

About the Author

Ryan has been married to Clarissa since 2011, and together they have two boys. They live in the beautiful city of Vancouver, WA in the Pacific Northwest. It is there that Ryan and his team started River City Church on Easter Sunday of 2019.

Ryan is continually amazed at the magnitude of what God is doing in their midst at River City Church!

We're at book 2, and that is still all that Ryan can think of to write about himself in the third person.